First Language English

for Cambridge IGCSE™

EXAM PREPARATION AND PRACTICE

Graham Elsdon & Helen Rees-Bidder

with Digital access

Shaftesbury Road, Cambridge CB2 8EA, United Kingdom

One Liberty Plaza, 20th Floor, New York, NY 10006, USA

477 Williamstown Road, Port Melbourne, VIC 3207, Australia

314–321, 3rd Floor, Plot 3, Splendor Forum, Jasola District Centre, New Delhi – 110025, India

Cambridge University Press & Assessment is a department of the University of Cambridge.

We share the University's mission to contribute to society through the pursuit of education, learning and research at the highest international levels of excellence.

www.cambridge.org
Information on this title: www.cambridge.org/9781009826419

First published 2026
20 19 18 17 16 15 14 13 12 11 10 9 8 7 6 5 4 3 2 1

Printed in the Netherlands by Wilco

A catalogue record for this publication is available from the British Library

ISBN 978-1-009-82641-9 Exam Preparation and Practice print with digital access
ISBN 978-1-009-82640-2 Digital Exam Preparation and Practice
ISBN 978-1-009-82642-6 Exam Preparation and Practice eBook

Additional resources for this publication at www.cambridge.org/go

For EU product safety concerns, contact us at Calle de José Abascal, 56, 1°, 28003 Madrid, Spain, or email eugpsr@cambridge.org.

2025 Cambridge Dedicated Teacher Awards

Our **Cambridge Dedicated Teacher Awards** are an opportunity to show appreciation for the incredible work teachers do every day.

Thank you to everyone who nominated this year; we have been inspired and moved by all of your stories. Well done to all of our nominees for your dedication to learning and for inspiring the next generation of thinkers, leaders and innovators.

Congratulations to our winners!

Global Winner
Sub-Saharan Africa

Portia Dzilah
Pakro-Adjinase St. James Anglican Basic School, Ghana

East Asia

Yun Xie
Yew Wah International Education School of Shanghai Lingang, China

Europe

Oleksandr Zhuk
Zaporizhzhia Special Comprehensive Boarding Xchool, Dzherelo, Ukraine

Latin America

Eduardo Pérez
Instituto Técnico Guaimaral, Colombia

North America

Isabel de Feria
Marjory Stoneman Douglas Elementary, USA

Middle East and North Africa

Farrukh Saleem
Pakistan International School Jeddah English Section, Saudi Arabia

Pakistan

Adnan Ahmed Usmani
Bahria Town School and College, Pakistan

South Asia

Sakina Bharmal
The Galaxy School - Wadi, India

Southeast Asia & Pacific

Polly Neville
Denla British School Bangkok, Thailand

or more information about our dedicated teachers and their stories, go to **dedicatedteacher.cambridge.org**

CAMBRIDGE

Contents

Digital questions for all chapters can be found online at Cambridge GO. For more information on how to access and use your digital resource, please see inside the front cover.

Note: Unit 6 of the Coursebook focuses on reading practice and is not included in this Exam Preparation and Practice.

> How to use this series

This suite of resources supports students and teachers following the Cambridge IGCSE™ and IGCSE (9-1) First Language English syllabuses (0500/0990). All of the components in the series are designed to work together and help students develop the necessary knowledge and skills for this subject.

The Coursebook is designed for students to use in class with guidance from the teacher. It is divided into two parts: reading and writing, and provides lots of opportunities for learners to develop these key skills through a range of engaging activities. Speaking and Listening tips offer different strategies to support learners in enhancing these skills while Reflection and Self-assessment features encourage learners to think about their own learning. Each unit ends with a Project and Practice questions that help consolidate learning.

A digital version of the Coursebook is included with the print version and is available separately.

The write-in Workbook consolidates the learning in the Coursebook by providing opportunities for more focused practice. It can be used flexibly, as an additional resource to support learning in the classroom or at home for individual work. The Workbook fully reflects the structure of the Coursebook, making it easy to navigate.

A digital version of the Workbook is included with the print version.

The Digital Teacher's Resource provides everything teachers need to deliver the course. It is packed full of useful teaching notes and lesson ideas, with suggestions for differentiation to support and challenge students, ideas for assessment, homework and project guidance.

A wide range of additional content such as worksheets, PowerPoint slides, end of unit tests, and answers to Coursebook and Workbook questions is also available to help teachers save time and enrich their practice.

The Exam Preparation and Practice* provides dedicated support for students as they work towards their final assessments. A wide range of questions and activities in the book and accompanying digital resource helps students consolidate knowledge, improve recall and respond more effectively. By focusing on command words, time management and mark allocation across exam papers, the materials build students' confidence and familiarity with exam language. Self-assessment and Reflection features support students to identify any areas that need further practice. This resource should be used alongside the Coursebook throughout the course of study.

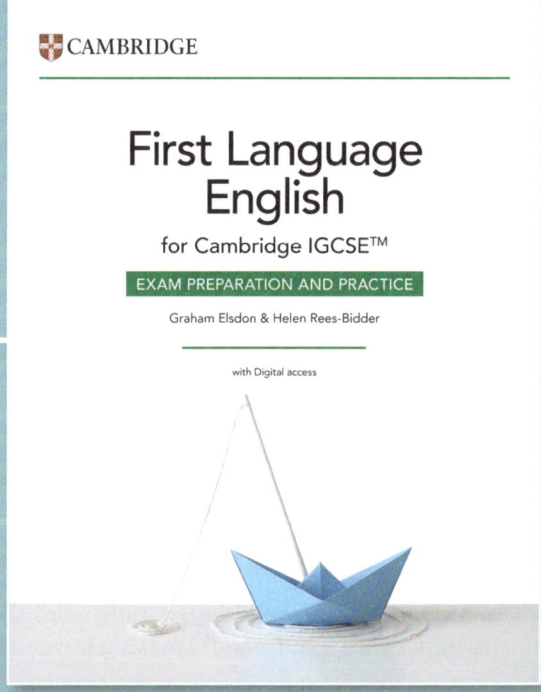

*This text has not been through the endorsement process for the Cambridge Pathway. Any references or materials related to answers, grades, papers or examinations are based on the opinion of the author(s). The Cambridge International Education syllabus assessment guidance material and specimen papers should always be referred to for definitive guidance.

› How to use this book

This book will help you to check that you **know** the content of the syllabus and practise how to **show** this understanding in an exam. It will also help you be cognitively prepared and in the **flow**, ready for your exam. Research has shown that it is important that you do all three of these things, so we have designed the Know, Show, Flow approach to help you prepare effectively for exams.

Know	You will need to consolidate and then recall a lot of syllabus content.

Show	You should demonstrate your knowledge in the context of a Cambridge exam.

Flow	You should be cognitively engaged and ready to learn. This means reducing test anxiety.

Exam skills checklist

Category	Exam skill
Understanding the question	Recognise different question types
	Understand command words
	Mark scheme awareness
Providing an appropriate response	Understand connections between concepts
	Keep to time
	Know what a good answer looks like
Developing supportive behaviours	Reflect on progress
	Manage test anxiety

This **Exam skills checklist** helps you to develop the awareness, behaviours and habits that will support you when revising and preparing for your exams. For more exam skills advice, including understanding command words and managing your time effectively, please go to the **Exam skills chapter**.

Know

The full syllabus content of your Cambridge IGCSE™ First Language English course is covered in your Cambridge Coursebook. This book will provide you with different types of questions to support you as you prepare for your exams. You will answer **Skills recall questions** that are designed to make sure you understand a topic, and **Recall and connect questions** to help you recall past learning and connect different concepts.

> ### SKILLS FOCUS
>
> Skills focus boxes summarise the topics that you will answer questions on in each unit of this book. You can refer back to your Cambridge Coursebook to remind yourself of the full detail of the syllabus content.

You will find **Skills recall questions** to make sure you understand a topic, and **Recall and connect questions** to help you recall past learning and connect different concepts. It is recommended that you answer the Skills recall questions just after you have covered the relevant topic in class, and then return to them at a later point to check you have properly understood the content.

Skills recall question

Testing yourself is a good way to check that your understanding is secure. These questions will help you to recall the core skills you have acquired during your course, and highlight any areas where you may need more practice. They are indicated with a blue bar with a gap, at the side of the page. We recommend that you answer the Skills recall questions just after you have covered the relevant topic in class, and then return to them at a later point to check you have properly understood the content.

> ### « RECALL AND CONNECT «
>
> To consolidate your learning, you need to test your memory frequently. These questions will test that you remember what you learnt in previous chapters, in addition to what you are practising in the current chapter.

> ### UNDERSTAND THIS TERM
>
> These list the important vocabulary that you should understand for each chapter. Definitions are provided in the glossary of your Cambridge Coursebook.

Show

Exam questions test specific knowledge, skills and understanding. You need to be prepared so that you have the best opportunity to show what you know in the time you have during the exam. In addition to practising recall of the syllabus content, it is important to build your exam skills throughout the year.

> **EXAM SKILLS FOCUS**
>
> This feature outlines the exam skills you will practise in each chapter, alongside the Knowledge focus. They are drawn from the core set of eight exam skills, listed in the exam skills checklist. You will practise specific exam skills, such as understanding command words, within each chapter. More general exam skills, such as managing text anxiety, are covered in the Exam skills chapter.

Exam skills question

These questions will help you to develop your exam skills and demonstrate your understanding. To help you become familiar with exam-style questioning, these questions follow the style and use the language of real exam questions, and have allocated marks. They are indicated with a solid red bar at the side of the page.

Looking at sample answers to past paper questions helps you to understand what to aim for.

The **Exam practice** sections in this resource contain example student responses and examiner-style commentary showing how the answer could be improved (both written by the authors).

Flow

Preparing for exams can be stressful. One of the approaches recommended by educational psychologists to help with this stress is to improve behaviours around exam preparation. This involves testing yourself in manageable chunks, accompanied by self-evaluation. You should avoid cramming, and build in more preparation time. This book is structured to help you do this.

Increasing your ability to recognise the signs of exam-related stress and working through some techniques for how to cope with it will help to make your exam preparation manageable.

REFLECTION

This feature asks you to think about the approach that you take to your exam preparation, and how you might improve this in the future. Reflecting on how you plan, monitor and evaluate your revision and preparation will help you to do your best in your exams.

SELF-ASSESSMENT CHECKLIST

These checklists return to the Learning intentions from your Coursebook, as well as the Exam skills focus boxes from each chapter. Checking in on how confident you feel in each of these areas will help you to focus your exam preparation. The 'Show it' prompts will allow you to test your rating. You should revisit any areas that you rate 'Needs more work' or 'Almost there'.

Now I can	Show it	Needs more work	Almost there	Confident to move on

Increasing your ability to recognise the signs of exam-related stress and working through some techniques for how to cope with it will help to make your exam preparation manageable. The **Exam skills chapter** will support you with this.

Digital questions

Extra digital questions, in the form of **Multiple choice** and **Flip cards**, for all chapters can be found online at Cambridge GO. For more information on how to access and use your digital resource, please see inside the front cover.

*   Provides lots of additional practice to reinforce knowledge and understanding

*   Gives instant feedback to support autonomy over your own learning

*   Encourages self-assessment to understand your strengths and weaknesses

*   User-friendly design to help with easy navigation

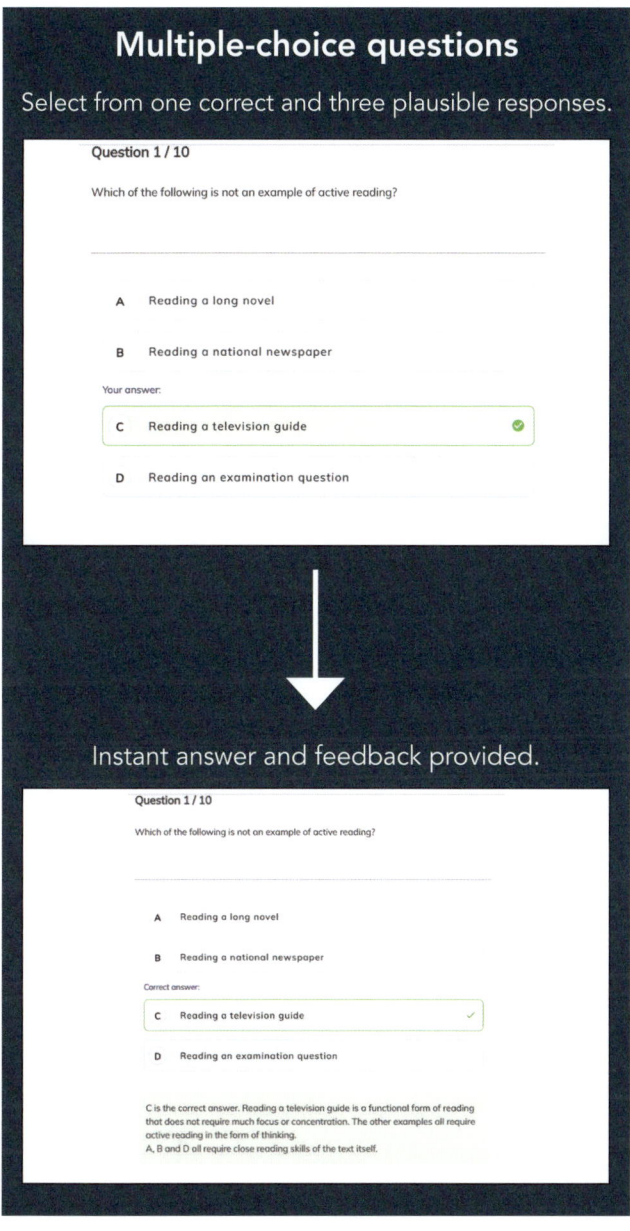

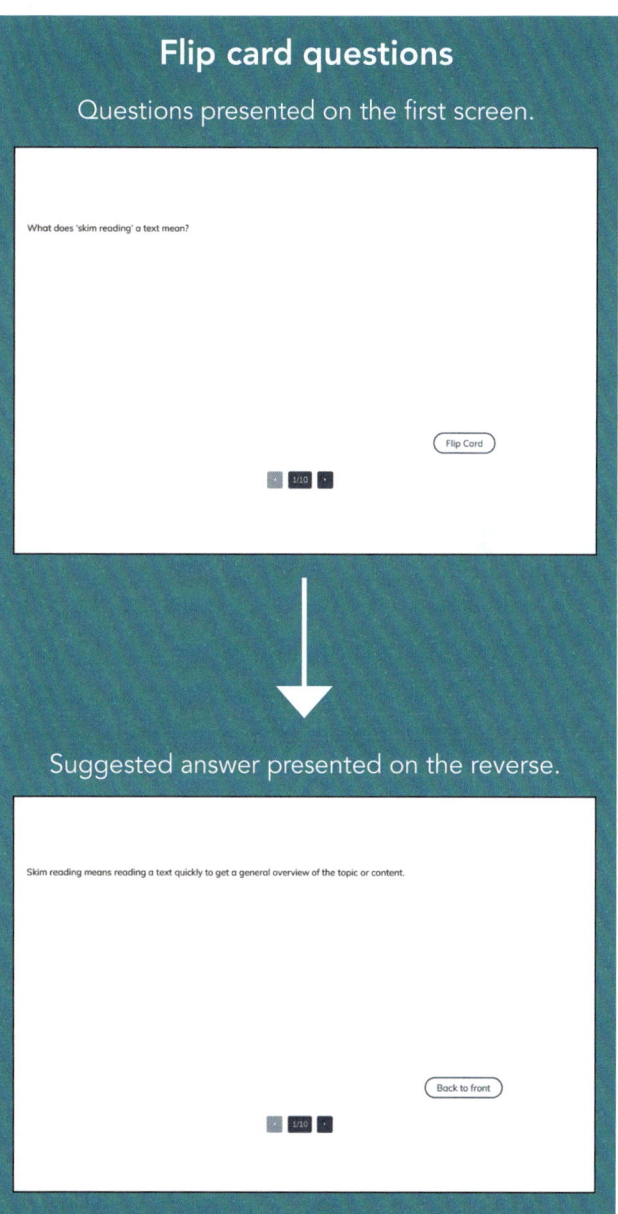

Syllabus assessment objectives for Cambridge IGCSE™ First Language English

You should be familiar with the Assessment Objectives from the syllabus, as you will need to show evidence of these requirements in your responses.

The assessment objectives for this syllabus are:

Assessment objective	IGCSE weighting
AO1: Reading	50%
AO2: Writing	50%
AO3: Speaking & Listening	Separately endorsed

Exam skills

by Lucy Parsons

What's the point of this book?

Most students make one really basic mistake when they're preparing for exams. What is it? It's focusing far too much on learning 'stuff' – that's facts, figures, ideas, information – and not nearly enough time practising exam skills.

The students who work really, really hard but are disappointed with their results are nearly always students who focus on memorising stuff. They think to themselves, 'I'll do practice papers once I've revised everything.' The trouble is, they start doing practice papers too late to really develop and improve how they communicate what they know.

What could they do differently?

When your final exam script is assessed, it should contain specific language, information and thinking skills in your answers. If you read a question in an exam and you have no idea what you need to do to give a good answer, the likelihood is that your answer won't be as brilliant as it could be. That means your grade won't reflect the hard work you've put into revising for the exam.

There are different types of questions used in exams to assess different skills. You need to know how to recognise these question types and understand what you need to show in your answers.

So, how do you understand what to do in each question type?

That's what this book is all about. But first a little background.

Meet Benjamin Bloom

The psychologist Benjamin Bloom developed a way of classifying and valuing different skills we use when we learn, such as analysis and recalling information. We call these thinking skills. It's known as Bloom's Taxonomy and it's what most exam questions are based around.

If you understand Bloom's Taxonomy, you can understand what any type of question requires you to do. So, what does it look like?

Bloom's Taxonomy of thinking skills

The key things to take away from this diagram are:

- Knowledge and understanding are known as lower-level thinking skills. They are less difficult than the other thinking skills. Exam questions that just test you on what you know are usually worth the lowest number of marks.

- All the other thinking skills are worth higher numbers of marks in exam questions. These questions need you to have some foundational knowledge and understanding but are far more about how you think than what you know. They involve:

  - Taking what you know and using it in unfamiliar situations (application).

  - Going deeper into information to discover relationships, motives, causes, patterns and connections (analysis).

  - Using what you know and think to create something new – whether that's an essay, long-answer exam question, a solution to a maths problem, or a piece of art (synthesis).

  - Assessing the value of something, e.g. the reliability of the results of a scientific experiment (evaluation).

In this introductory chapter, you'll be shown how to develop the skills that enable you to communicate what you know and how you think. This will help you achieve to the best of your abilities. In the rest of the book, you'll have a chance to practise these exam skills by understanding how questions work and understanding what you need to show in your answers.

Every time you pick up this book and do a few questions, you're getting closer to achieving your dream results. So, let's get started!

Exam preparation and revision skills

What is revision?

If you think about it, the word 'revision' has two parts to it:

- re – which means 'again'

- vision – which is about seeing.

So, revision is literally about 'seeing again'. This means you're looking at something that you've already learnt.

Typically, a teacher will teach you something in class. You may then do some questions on it, write about it in some way, or even do a presentation. You might then have an end-of-topic test sometime later. To prepare for this test, you need to 'look again' or revise what you were originally taught.

Step 1: Making knowledge stick

Every time you come back to something you've learnt or revised you're improving your understanding and memory of that particular piece of knowledge. This is called **spaced retrieval**. This is how human memory works. If you don't use a piece of knowledge by recalling it, you lose it.

Everything we learn has to be physically stored in our brains by creating neural connections – joining brain cells together. The more often we 'retrieve' or recall a particular piece of knowledge, the stronger the neural connection gets. It's like lifting weights – the more often you lift, the stronger you get.

However, if you don't use a piece of knowledge for a long time, your brain wants to recycle the brain cells and use them for another purpose. The neural connections get weaker until they finally break, and the memory has gone. This is why it's really important to return often to things that you've learnt in the past.

Great ways of doing this in your revision include:

- Testing yourself using flip cards – use the ones available in the digital resources for this book.

- Testing yourself (or getting someone else to test you) using questions you've created about the topic.

- Checking your recall of previous topics by answering the Recall and connect questions in this book.

- Blurting – writing everything you can remember about a topic on a piece of paper in one colour. Then, checking what you missed out and filling it in with another colour. You can do this over and over again until you feel confident that you remember everything.

- Answering practice questions – use the ones in this book.

- Getting a good night's sleep to help consolidate your learning.

> **The importance of sleep and creating long-term memory**
>
> When you go to sleep at night, your brain goes through an important process of taking information from your short-term memory and storing it in your long-term memory.
>
> This means that getting a good night's sleep is a very important part of revision. If you don't get enough good quality sleep, you'll actually be making your revision much, much harder.

Step 2: Developing your exam skills

We've already talked about the importance of exam skills, and how many students neglect them because they're worried about covering all the knowledge.

What actually works best is developing your exam skills at the same time as learning the knowledge.

What does this look like in your studies?

- Learning something at school and your teacher setting you questions from this book or from past papers. This tests your recall as well as developing your exam skills.

- Choosing a topic to revise, learning the content and then choosing some questions from this book to test yourself at the same time as developing your exam skills.

The reason why practising your exam skills is so important is that it helps you to get good at communicating what you know and what you think. The more often you do that, the more fluent you'll become in showing what you know in your answers.

Step 3: Getting feedback

The final step is to get feedback on your work.

If you're testing yourself, the feedback is what you got wrong or what you forgot. This means you then need to go back to those things to remind yourself or improve your understanding. Then, you can test yourself again and get more feedback. You can also congratulate yourself for the things you got right – it's important to celebrate any success, big or small.

If you're doing past paper questions or the practice questions in this book, you will need to mark your work. Marking your work is one of the most important things you can do to improve. It's possible to make significant improvements in your marks in a very short space of time when you start marking your work.

Why is marking your own work so powerful? It's because it teaches you to identify the strengths and weaknesses of your own work. When you look at the mark scheme and see how it's structured, you will understand what is needed in your answers to get the results you want.

This doesn't just apply to the knowledge you demonstrate in your answers. It also applies to the language you use and whether it's appropriately subject-specific, the structure of your answer, how you present it on the page and many other factors. Understanding, practising and improving on these things are transformative for your results.

The most important thing about revision

The most important way to make your revision successful is to make it active.

Sometimes, students say they're revising when they sit staring at their textbook or notes for hours at a time. However, this is a really ineffective way to revise because it's passive. In order to make knowledge and skills stick, you need to be doing something like the suggestions in the following diagram. That's why testing yourself and pushing yourself to answer questions that test higher-level thinking skills are so effective. At times, you might actually be able to feel the physical changes happening in your brain as you develop this new knowledge and these new skills. That doesn't come about without effort.

The important thing to remember is that while active revision feels much more like hard work than passive revision, you don't actually need to do nearly as much of it. That's because you remember knowledge and skills when you use active revision. When you use passive revision, it is much, much harder for the knowledge and skills to stick in your memory.

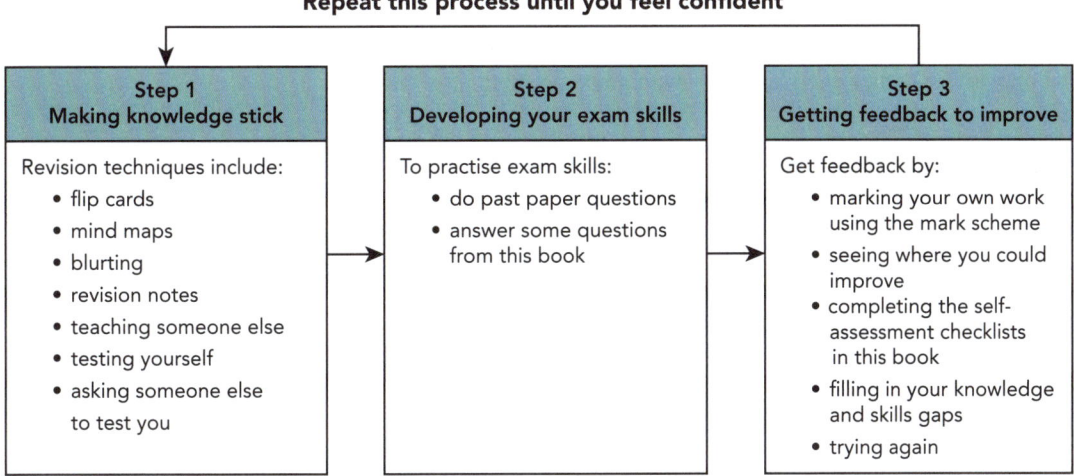

Repeat this process until you feel confident

Step 1 Making knowledge stick	Step 2 Developing your exam skills	Step 3 Getting feedback to improve
Revision techniques include: • flip cards • mind maps • blurting • revision notes • teaching someone else • testing yourself • asking someone else to test you	To practise exam skills: • do past paper questions • answer some questions from this book	Get feedback by: • marking your own work using the mark scheme • seeing where you could improve • completing the self-assessment checklists in this book • filling in your knowledge and skills gaps • trying again

How to improve your exam skills

This book helps you to improve in eight different areas of exam skills, which are divided across three categories. These skills are highlighted in this book in the Exam skills focus at the start of each chapter and developed throughout the book using targeted questions, advice and reflections.

1 **Understand the questions: what are you being asked to do?**

- Know your question types.

- Understand command words.

- Work with mark scheme awareness.

2 **How to answer questions brilliantly**

- Understand connections between concepts.

- Keep to time.

- Know what a good answer looks like.

3 **Give yourself the best chance of success**

- Reflection on progress.

- How to manage test anxiety.

Understand the questions: what are you being asked to do?

Know your question types

In any exam, there will be a range of different question types. These different question types will test different types of thinking skills from Bloom's Taxonomy.

It is very important that you learn to recognise different question types. If you do lots of past papers, over time you will begin to recognise the structure of the paper for each of your subjects. You will know which types of questions may come first and which ones are more likely to come at the end of the paper. You can also complete past paper questions in the Exam practice sections in this book for additional practice.

You will also recognise the differences between questions worth a lower number of marks and questions worth more marks. The key differences are:

- how much you will need to write in your answer

- how sophisticated your answer needs to be in terms of the detail you give and the depth of thinking you show.

Types of questions

1   **Multiple-choice questions**

   Multiple-choice questions are generally worth smaller numbers of marks. You will be given several possible answers to the question, and you will have to work out which one is correct using your knowledge and skills.

   There is a chance of you getting the right answer with multiple-choice questions even if you don't know the answer. This is why you must **always give an answer for multiple-choice questions** as it means there is a chance you will earn the mark.

   Multiple-choice questions are often harder than they appear. The possible answers can be very similar to each other. This means you must be confident in how you work out answers or have a high level of understanding to tell the difference between the possible answers.

   Being confident in your subject knowledge and doing lots of practice multiple-choice questions will set you up for success. Use the resources in this book and the accompanying online resources to build your confidence.

   This example of a multiple-choice question is worth one mark. You can see that all the answers have one part in common with at least one other answer. For example, palisade cells is included in three of the possible answers. That's why you have to really know the detail of your content knowledge to do well with multiple-choice questions.

   Which two types of cells are found in plant leaves?

   A   Palisade mesophyll and stomata

   B   Palisade mesophyll and root hair

   C   Stomata and chloroplast

   D   Chloroplast and palisade mesophyll

2 Questions requiring longer-form answers

Questions requiring longer-form answers need you to write out your answer yourself.

With these questions, take careful note of how many marks are available and how much space you've been given for your answer. These two things will give you a good idea about how much you should say and how much time you should spend on the question.

A rough rule to follow is to write one sentence, or make one point, for each mark that is available. You will get better and better at these longer form questions the more you practise them.

In this example of a history question, you can see it is worth four marks. It is not asking for an explanation, just for you to list Lloyd George's aims. Therefore, you need to make four correct points in order to get full marks.

What were Lloyd George's aims during negotiations leading to the
Treaty of Versailles?   [4]

3 Essay questions

Essay questions are the longest questions you will be asked to answer in an exam. They examine the higher-order thinking skills from Bloom's Taxonomy such as analysis, synthesis and evaluation.

To do well in essay questions, you need to talk about what you know, giving your opinion, comparing one concept or example to another, and evaluating your own ideas or the ones you're discussing in your answer.

You also need to have a strong structure and logical argument that guides the reader through your thought process. This usually means having an introduction, some main body paragraphs that discuss one point at a time, and a conclusion.

Essay questions are usually level-marked. This means that you don't get one mark per point you make. Instead, you're given marks for the quality of the ideas you're sharing as well as how well you present those ideas through the subject-specific language you use and the structure of your essay.

Practising essays and becoming familiar with the mark scheme is the only way to get really good at them.

Understand command words

What are command words?

Command words are the most important words in every exam question. This is because command words tell you what you need to do in your answer. Do you remember Bloom's Taxonomy? Command words tell you which thinking skill you need to demonstrate in the answer to each question.

Two very common command words are **describe** and **explain**.

When you see the command word describe in a question, you're being asked to show lower-order thinking skills like knowledge and understanding. The question will either be worth fewer marks, or you will need to make more points if it is worth more marks.

The command word explain is asking you to show higher-order thinking skills. When you see the command word explain, you need to be able to say how or why something happens.

You need to understand all of the relevant command words for the subjects you are taking. Ask your teacher where to find them if you are not sure. It's best not to try to memorise the list of command words, but to become familiar with what command words are asking for by doing lots of practice questions and marking your own work.

How to work with command words

When you first see an exam question, read it through once. Then, read it through again and identify the command word(s). Underline the command word(s) to make it clear to yourself which they are every time you refer back to the question.

You may also want to identify the **content** words in the question and underline them with a different colour. Content words tell you which area of knowledge you need to draw on to answer the question.

In this example, command words are shown in red and underlined with content words in **blue and bold**:

1 a Explain **four** reasons why **governments** might **support business start-ups**. [8]

   Adapted from Cambridge IGCSE Business Studies (0450)
   Q1a Paper 21 June 2022

Marking your own work using the mark scheme will help you get even better at understanding command words and knowing how to give good answers for each.

Work with mark scheme awareness

The most transformative thing that any student can do to improve their marks is to work with mark schemes. This means using mark schemes to mark your own work at every opportunity.

Many students are very nervous about marking their own work as they do not feel experienced or qualified enough. However, being brave enough to try to mark your own work and taking the time to get good at it will improve your marks hugely.

Why marking your own work makes such a big difference

Marking your own work can help you to improve your answers in the following ways:

1 **Answering the question**

   Having a deep and detailed understanding of what is required by the question enables you to answer the question more clearly and more accurately.

   It can also help you to give the required information using fewer words and in less time, as you can avoid including unrelated points or topics in your answer.

2 **Using subject-specific vocabulary**

   Every subject has subject-specific vocabulary. This includes technical terms for objects or concepts in a subject, such as mitosis and meiosis in biology. It also includes how you talk about the subject, using appropriate vocabulary that may differ from everyday language. For example, in any science subject you might be asked to describe the trend on a graph.

   Your answer could say it 'goes up fast' or your answer could say it 'increases rapidly'. You would not get marks for saying it 'goes up fast', but you would for saying it 'increases rapidly'. This is the difference between everyday language and formal, scientific language.

When you answer lots of practice questions, you become fluent in the language specific to your subject.

3 Knowing how much to write

It's very common for students to either write too much or too little to answer questions. Becoming familiar with the mark schemes for many different questions will help you to gain a better understanding of how much you need to write in order to get a good mark.

4 Structuring your answer

There are often clues in questions about how to structure your answer. However, mark schemes give you an even stronger idea of the structure you should use in your answers.

For example, if a question says:

'Describe and explain two reasons why…'

You can give a clear answer by:

- Describing reason 1
- Explaining reason 1
- Describing reason 2
- Explaining reason 2.

Having a very clear structure will also make it easier to identify where you have earned marks. This means that you're more likely to be awarded the number of marks you deserve.

5 Keeping to time

Answering the question, using subject-specific vocabulary, knowing how much to write and giving a clear structure to your answer will all help you to keep to time in an exam. You will not waste time by writing too much for any answer. Therefore, you will have sufficient time to give a good answer to every question.

How to answer exam questions brilliantly

Understand connections between concepts

One of the higher-level thinking skills in Bloom's Taxonomy is **synthesis**. Synthesis means making connections between different areas of knowledge. You may have heard about synoptic links. Making synoptic links is the same as showing the thinking skill of synthesis.

Exam questions that ask you to show your synthesis skills are usually worth the highest number of marks on an exam paper. To write good answers to these questions, you need to spend time thinking about the links between the topics you've studied before you arrive in your exam. A great way of doing this is using mind maps.

How to create a mind map

To create a mind map:

1 Use a large piece of paper and several different coloured pens.

2   Write the name of your subject in the middle. Then, write the key topic areas evenly spaced around the edge, each with a different colour.

3   Then, around each topic area, start to write the detail of what you can remember. If you find something that is connected with something you studied in another topic, you can draw a line linking the two things together.

This is a good way of practising your retrieval of information as well as linking topics together.

Answering synoptic exam questions

You will recognise questions that require you to make links between concepts because they have a higher number of marks. You will have practised them using this book and the accompanying resources.

To answer a synoptic exam question:

1   **Identify the command and content words**. You are more likely to find command words like **discuss** and **explain** in these questions. They might also have phrases like 'the connection between'.

2   **Make a plan for your answer**. It is worth taking a short amount of time to think about what you're going to write in your answer. Think carefully about what information you're going to put in, the links between the different pieces of information and how you're going to structure your answer to make your ideas clear.

3   **Use linking words and phrases in your answer**. For example, 'therefore', 'because', due to', 'since' or 'this means that'.

Here is an example of an English Literature exam question that requires you to make synoptic links in your answer.

1   Discuss **Carol Ann Duffy's exploration of childhood** in her poetry.

Refer to **two** poems in your answer.   [25]

Content words are shown in blue; command words are shown in red.

This question is asking you to explore the theme of childhood in Duffy's poetry. You need to choose two of her poems to refer to in your answer. This means you need a good knowledge of her poetry, and to be familiar with her exploration of childhood, so that you can easily select two poems that will give you plenty to say in your answer.

Keep to time

Managing your time in exams is really important. Some students do not achieve to the best of their abilities because they run out of time to answer all the questions. However, if you manage your time well, you will be able to attempt every question on the exam paper.

Why is it important to attempt all the questions on an exam paper?

If you attempt every question on a paper, you have the best chance of achieving the highest mark you are capable of.

Students who manage their time poorly in exams will often spend far too long on some questions and not even attempt others. Most students are unlikely to get full marks on many questions, but you will get zero marks for the questions you don't answer. You can maximise your marks by giving an answer to every question.

Minutes per mark

The most important way to keep to time is knowing how many minutes you can spend on each mark.

For example, if your exam paper has 90 marks available and you have 90 minutes, you know there is 1 mark per minute.

Therefore, if you have a 5 mark question, you should spend five minutes on it.

Sometimes, you can give a good answer in less time than you have budgeted using the minutes per mark technique. If this happens, you will have more time to spend on questions that use higher-order thinking skills, or more time on checking your work.

How to get faster at answering exam questions

The best way to get faster at answering exam questions is to do lots of practice. You should practise each question type that will be in your exam, marking your own work, so that you know precisely how that question works and what is required by the question. Use the questions in this book to get better and better at answering each question type.

Use the 'Slow, Slow, Quick' technique to get faster.

Take your time answering questions when you first start practising them. You may answer them with the support of the textbook, your notes or the mark scheme. These things will support you with your content knowledge, the language you use in your answer and the structure of your answer.

Every time you practise this question type, you will get more confident and faster. You will become experienced with this question type, so that it is easy for you to recall the subject knowledge and write it down using the correct language and a good structure.

Calculating marks per minute

Use this calculation to work out how long you have for each mark:

Total time in the exam / Number of marks available = Minutes per mark

Calculate how long you have for a question worth more than one mark like this:

Minutes per mark × Marks available for this question
= Number of minutes for this question

What about time to check your work?

It is a very good idea to check your work at the end of an exam. You need to work out if this is feasible with the minutes per mark available to you. If you're always rushing to finish the questions, you shouldn't budget checking time. However, if you usually have time to spare, then you can budget checking time.

To include checking time in your minutes per mark calculation:

(Total time in the exam – Checking time) / Number of marks available
= Minutes per mark

Know what a good answer looks like

It is much easier to give a good answer if you know what a good answer looks like.

Use these methods to know what a good answer looks like.

1 **Sample answers** – you can find sample answers in these places:

- from your teacher
- written by your friends or other members of your class
- in this book.

2 **Look at mark schemes** – mark schemes are full of information about what you should include in your answers. Get familiar with mark schemes to gain a better understanding of the type of things a good answer would contain.

3 **Feedback from your teacher** – if you are finding it difficult to improve your exam skills for a particular type of question, ask your teacher for detailed feedback. You should also look at their comments on your work in detail.

Give yourself the best chance of success

Reflection on progress

As you prepare for your exam, it's important to reflect on your progress. Taking time to think about what you're doing well and what could be improved brings more focus to your revision. Reflecting on progress also helps you to continuously improve your knowledge and exam skills.

How do you reflect on progress?

Use the 'reflection' feature in this book to help you reflect on your progress during your exam preparation. Then, at the end of each revision session, take a few minutes to think about the following:

	What went well? What would you do the same next time?	What didn't go well? What would you do differently next time?
Your subject knowledge		
How you revised your subject knowledge – did you use active retrieval techniques?		
Your use of subject-specific and academic language		
Understanding the question by identifying command words and content words		
Giving a clear structure to your answer		
Keeping to time		
Marking your own work		

Remember to check for silly mistakes – things like missing the units out after you carefully calculated your answer.

Use the mark scheme to mark your own work. Every time you mark your own work, you will be recognising the good and bad aspects of your work, so that you can progressively give better answers over time.

When do you need to come back to this topic or skill?

Earlier in this section of the book, we talked about revision skills and the importance of spaced retrieval. When you reflect on your progress, you need to think about how soon you need to return to the topic or skill you've just been focusing on.

For example, if you were really disappointed with your subject knowledge, it would be a good idea to do some more active retrieval and practice questions on this topic tomorrow. However, if you did really well, you can feel confident you know this topic and come back to it again in three weeks' or a month's time.

The same goes for exam skills. If you were disappointed with how you answered the question, you should look at some sample answers and try this type of question again soon. However, if you did well, you can move on to other types of exam questions.

Improving your memory of subject knowledge

Sometimes students slip back into using passive revision techniques, such as only reading the Coursebook or their notes, rather than also using active revision techniques, like testing themselves using flip cards or blurting.

You can avoid this mistake by observing how well your learning is working as you revise. You should be thinking to yourself, 'Am I remembering this? Am I understanding this? Is this revision working?'

If the answer to any of those questions is 'no', then you need to change what you're doing to revise this particular topic. For example, if you don't understand, you could look up your topic in a different textbook in the school library to see if a different explanation helps. Or you could see if you can find a video online that brings the idea to life.

You are in control

When you're studying for exams it's easy to think that your teachers are in charge. However, you have to remember that you are studying for your exams and the results you get will be yours and no one else's.

That means you have to take responsibility for all your exam preparation. You have the power to change how you're preparing if what you're doing isn't working. You also have control over what you revise and when: you can make sure you focus on your weaker topics and skills to improve your achievement in the subject.

This isn't always easy to do. Sometimes you have to find an inner ability that you have not used before. But, if you are determined enough to do well, you can find what it takes to focus, improve and keep going.

What is test anxiety?

Do you get worried or anxious about exams? Does your worry or anxiety impact how well you do in tests and exams?

Test anxiety is part of your natural stress response.

The stress response evolved in animals and humans many thousands of years ago to help keep them alive. Let's look at an example.

The stress response in the wild

Imagine an impala grazing in the grasslands of east Africa. It's happily and calmly eating grass in its herd in what we would call the parasympathetic state of rest and repair.

Then the impala sees a lion. The impala suddenly panics because its life is in danger. This state of panic is also known as the stressed or sympathetic state. The sympathetic state presents itself in three forms: flight, fight and freeze.

The impala starts to run away from the lion. Running away is known as the flight stress response.

The impala might not be fast enough to run away from the lion. The lion catches it but has a loose grip. The impala struggles to try to get away. This struggle is the fight stress response.

However, the lion gets an even stronger grip on the impala. Now the only chance of the impala surviving is playing dead. The impala goes limp, its heart rate and breathing slows. This is called the freeze stress response. The lion believes that it has killed the impala so it drops the impala to the ground. Now the impala can switch back into the flight response and run away.

The impala is now safe – the different stages of the stress response have saved its life.

What has the impala got to do with your exams?

When you feel test anxiety, you have the same physiological stress responses as an impala being hunted by a lion. Unfortunately, the human nervous system cannot tell the difference between a life-threatening situation, such as being chased by a lion, and the stress of taking an exam.

If you understand how the stress response works in the human nervous system, you will be able to learn techniques to reduce test anxiety.

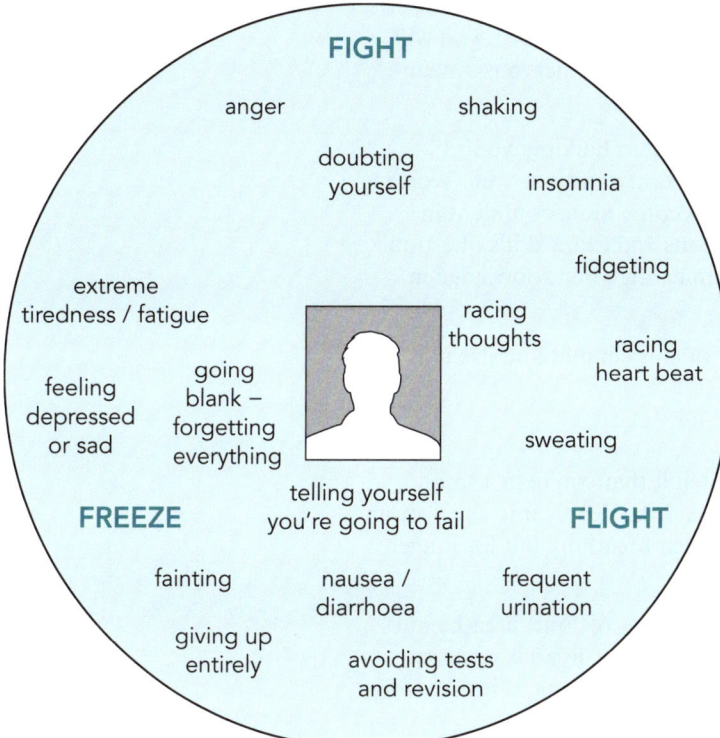

The role of the vagus nerve in test anxiety

The vagus nerve is the part of your nervous system that determines your stress response. Vagus means 'wandering' in Latin, so the vagus nerve is also known as the 'wandering nerve'. The vagus nerve wanders from your brain, down each side of your body, to nearly all your organs, including your lungs, heart, kidneys, liver, digestive system and bladder.

If you are in a stressful situation, like an exam, your vagus nerve sends a message to all these different organs to activate their stress response. Here are some common examples:

*   **Heart** beats faster.

*   **Kidneys** produce more adrenaline so that you can run, making you fidgety and distracted.

*   **Digestive system** and **bladder** want to eliminate all waste products so that energy can be used for fight or flight.

If you want to feel calmer about your revision and exams, you need to do two things to help you move into the parasympathetic, or rest and repair, state:

1 Work with your vagus nerve to send messages of safety through your body.

2 Change your perception of the test so that you see it as safe and not dangerous.

How to cope with test anxiety

1 Be well prepared

Good preparation is the most important part of managing test anxiety. The better your preparation, the more confident you will be. If you are confident, you will not perceive the test or exam as dangerous, so the sympathetic nervous system responses of fight, flight and freeze are less likely to happen.

This book is all about helping you to be well prepared and building your confidence in your knowledge and ability to answer exam questions well. Working through the skills recall questions will help you to become more confident in your knowledge of the subject. The practice questions and exam skills questions will help you to become more confident in communicating your knowledge in an exam.

To be well prepared, look at the advice in the rest of this chapter and use it as you work through the questions in this book.

2 Work with your vagus nerve

The easiest way to work with your vagus nerve to tell it that you're in a safe situation is through your breathing. This means breathing deeply into the bottom of your lungs, so that your stomach expands, and then breathing out for longer than you breathed in. You can do this with counting.

Breathe in deeply, expanding your abdomen, for the count of four; breathe out drawing your navel back towards your spine for the count of five, six or seven. Repeat this at least three times. However, you can do it for as long as it takes for you to feel calm.

The important thing is that you breathe out for longer than you breathe in. This is because when you breathe in, your heart rate increases slightly, and when you breathe out, your heart rate decreases slightly. If you're spending more time breathing out overall, you will be decreasing your heart rate over time.

3 Feel it

Anxiety is an uncomfortable, difficult thing to feel. That means that many people try to run away from anxious feelings. However, this means the stress just gets stored in your body for you to feel later.

When you feel anxious, follow these four steps:

1 Pause.

2 Place one hand on your heart and one hand on your stomach.

3 Notice what you're feeling.

4 Stay with your feelings.

What you will find is that if you are willing to experience what you feel for a minute or two, the feeling of anxiety will usually pass very quickly.

4   Write or talk it out

If your thoughts are moving very quickly, it is often better to get them out of your mind and on to paper.

You could take a few minutes to write down everything that comes through your mind, then rip up your paper and throw it away. If you don't like writing, you can speak aloud alone or to someone you trust.

Other ways to break the stress cycle

Exercise and movement	Being friendly	Laughter
• Run or walk. • Dance. • Lift weights. • Yoga. Anything that involves moving your body is helpful.	• Chat to someone in your study break. • Talk to the cashier when you buy your lunch.	• Watch or listen to a funny show on TV or online. • Talk with someone who makes you laugh. • Look at photos of fun times.
Have a hug • Hug a friend or relative. • Cuddle a pet, e.g. a cat. Hug for 20 seconds or until you feel calm and relaxed.	**Releasing emotions** It is healthy to release negative or sad emotions. Crying is often a quick way to get rid of these difficult feelings so if you feel like you need to cry, allow it.	**Creativity** • Paint, draw or sketch. • Sew, knit or crochet. • Cook, build something.

If you have long-term symptoms of anxiety, it is important to tell someone you trust and ask for help.

Your perfect revision session

1 **Intention**

What do you want to achieve in this revision session?
- Choose an area of knowledge or an exam skill that you want to focus on.
- Choose some questions from this book that focus on this knowledge area or skill.
- Gather any other resources you will need, e.g. pen, paper, flashcards, Coursebook.

2 **Focus**

Set your focus for the session
- Remove distractions from your study area, e.g. leave your phone in another room.
- Write down on a piece of paper or sticky note the knowledge area or skill you're intending to focus on.
- Close your eyes and take three deep breaths, with the exhale longer than the inhale.

3 **Revision**

Revise your knowledge and understanding
- To improve your knowledge and understanding of the topic, use your Coursebook, notes or flashcards, including active learning techniques.
- To improve your exam skills, look at previous answers, teacher feedback, mark schemes, sample answers or examiners' reports.

4 **Practice**

Answer practice questions
- Use the questions in this book, or in the additional online resources, to practise your exam skills.
- If the exam is soon, do this in timed conditions without the support of the Coursebook or your notes.
- If the exam is a long time away, you can use your notes and resources to help you.

5 **Feedback**

Mark your answers
- Use mark schemes to mark your work.
- Reflect on what you've done well and what you could do to improve next time.

6 **Next steps**

What have you learnt about your progress from this revision session? What do you need to do next?
- What did you do well? Feel good about these things, and know it's safe to set these things aside for a while.
- What do you need to work on? How are you going to improve? Make a plan to get better at the things you didn't do well or didn't know.

7 **Rest**

Take a break
- Do something completely different to rest: get up, move or do something creative or practical.
- Remember that rest is an important part of studying, as it gives your brain a chance to integrate your learning.

Reading

1 Reading skills and strategies

In this unit you will explore a range of different types of questions that you may come across in the assessment. As you read a variety of texts actively, you will apply independent reading strategies to show your comprehension of texts in response to these different question types.

1.1 An introduction to reading skills

Reading in examinations is an active process – you need to really think about what a text is saying to get as much out of it as you can. It is important to practise your active reading skills so you can demonstrate a full understanding of the texts on which you are assessed.

1 Read Text 1.1.

  a Write down the purpose of the text.

  b Make a note of any words or phrases you do not understand and check their meanings.

  c Write a **one**-sentence summary of each paragraph.

> **Text 1.1**
>
> Unlock a hidden world of shifting landscapes and unparalleled beauty as you journey onboard the award-winning Rocky Mountaineer train.
>
> The Rocky Mountaineer train offers three spellbinding Canadian routes through the Rockies to choose from, each with its own distinctive highlights. Plus discover the new USA route, Rockies to the Red Rocks. 5
>
> Carve through areas unreachable by road and witness the mesmerising beauty of the majestic mountain ranges and the remote vistas. Relax in luxury and indulge all your senses onboard the all-dome fleet as you enjoy gourmet cuisine, impeccable service, historic storytelling, and breathtaking scenery. 10
>
> [...]
>
> Let us help create a Canada holiday including this once-in-a-lifetime trip just for you. Contact our travel experts for further details.
>
> From mycanadatrips.co.uk

2 Write **three** questions that would test a reader's understanding of Text 1.1. Note down the answers on a separate piece of paper. Swap questions with a partner and write down the answers in your notebook, then check each other's comprehension skills.

1.2 Reading strategies

When responding to unseen texts in the examination, you will have to decide which reading strategy will best help you to locate, select and use the information you need in order to answer the different types of questions.

Identifying the most appropriate reading strategy will ensure that you use your time wisely, and work through the questions quickly and efficiently. You may need to scan a text to form an overview of what it is about, or if you are responding to a short question asking for explicit meaning, you may use a reading strategy such as skim reading to quickly locate information. For other question types, such as when

> **TIP**
>
> Always read a text carefully before you look at any questions associated with it. This will ensure that you understand the gist of the text – what it is about and the writer's intentions.

> **UNDERSTAND THIS TERM**
>
> • gist

> **UNDERSTAND THESE TERMS**
>
> • skim
> • scan

considering writer's effects, you need to read more closely to successfully analyse the language.

1   a   Skim read Text 1.2 and explain what it is about in **one** sentence.

    b   Scan the text and make a list of the advantages of the monsoon season.

    c   Scan the text and make a list of the disadvantages of the monsoon season.

Text 1.2

In India, the monsoon season starts in late June and lasts until September, with torrential rain falling every day. When the wind and rain start, they are a relief from the stifling summer heat, but as the weeks go on, the waterlogged streets, traffic jams and landslides become a heavy price to pay.   5

Seventy per cent of India's rainfall comes from the monsoon season, which is essential for agriculture in a country prone to droughts and with a poor record of water conservation. The rainfall fills up rivers and lakes, as well as nourishing the soil to produce healthy crops. A good monsoon correlates with a booming economy, whereas a poor monsoon results in a   10
poor harvest and poor economic growth. About 60% of India's agricultural land wholly depends on rain for its water due to a lack of irrigation.

The heavy rains also lead to increased electricity production from hydropower plants, which provide electricity and water supplies to cities. On the whole, however, urban dwellers endure more disruption   15
caused by monsoon rains as floods cause damage to buildings and infrastructure. Even the commute to work can become hazardous, disrupting daily life and affecting productivity. For example, floods between June and September in 2021 led to economic losses of over $3 billion. Those living in temporary slum dwellings suffer most, as their   20
flimsy housing often collapses in heavy rain. There are also public health risks due to mosquitoes breeding in the damp conditions and spreading diseases such as dengue and malaria.

On a brighter note, the environment undergoes a transformation in the monsoon season. The rains wash away the dust, and barren valleys with   25
dried-up streams transform into vibrant landscapes alive with shades of green. Some areas of India have started to promote monsoon tourism, in which tourists are offered unique and adventurous experiences in diverse landscapes featuring lush rainforests, scenic hill stations and the Himalayan mountains.   30

Reading inferentially means working out what a writer is implying or suggesting in a text, by carefully examining their language choices. When you give an answer that shows something you have inferred, you should always provide evidence from the text to support your ideas.

UNDERSTAND THESE TERMS

- infer
- imply

2 Read Text 1.2 again, this time more closely.

    a What does the word 'stifling' in paragraph 1 suggest about the summer heat?

    b Give **two** things that could be done to help farmers in India rely less on the monsoon rains, according to paragraph 2.

    c Give **two** ways that living in a city becomes more dangerous during the monsoon season.

    d Does the writer suggest that life is better in rural areas or urban areas during the monsoon season? Support your answer with details from the text.

1.3 Types of texts

It is important to recognise the different types of texts you may have to read and respond to in an exam. Identifying the type of text that you are reading will help you to understand its purpose and intended audience, as well as to identify and analyse key features of the writing.

An unseen text may be fiction or non-fiction, but within these categories there are other genres with which you should familiarise yourself.

Text 1.3 is an informative text about the development of the internet.

> **UNDERSTAND THESE TERMS**
> - fiction
> - non-fiction
> - genre

Text 1.3

The internet as we know it today was invented in 1990 by Tim Berners-Lee, a British computer scientist. It was called the World Wide Web and was simply a system of hyperlinked documents that could be accessed by computer owners if they also had a modem. In reality, very few people owned a household computer in 1990 – and even fewer owned a modem. It is estimated that in the USA only   5 about 15% of homes had a computer, and in countries like the UK it was less than 10%. Modem ownership was even more rare.

At first, the growth of the World Wide Web was relatively slow: by 1992 there were just a few hundred websites. However, in 1993 the first graphical web browser, Mosaic, was launched and, for the first time, images and texts could be   10 viewed alongside one another. This opened up all kinds of possibilities for users to design eye-catching websites; it also offered an unlimited range of commercial opportunities. This led to the creation of search engines such as Yahoo, and by 1996 online businesses such as Amazon and eBay were founded. By the end of 1995, the number of internet users globally was estimated to be in excess of   15 40 million.

> **TIP**
>
> In the exam, you are most likely to come across informative texts, articles, journals, letters, speeches, biographical accounts and narrative stories. Usually, Texts A and B are non-fiction, and Text C is fiction or literary non-fiction in the form of a narrative account.

Text 1.4 is an extract from a newspaper article about the development of the internet.

Text 1.4

Forty years of the internet: how the world changed for ever

I have no recollection of when I first used the world wide web, though it was
almost certainly when people still called it the world wide web, or even W3,
perhaps in the same breath as the phrase "information superhighway", made
popular by Al Gore. (Or "infobahn": did any of us really, ever, call the internet the
"infobahn"?) For most of us, though, the web is in effect synonymous with the   5
internet, even if we grasp that in technical terms that's inaccurate: the web is simply
a system that sits on top of the internet, making it greatly easier to navigate the
information there, and to use it as a medium of sharing and communication. But
the distinction rarely seems relevant in everyday life now, which is why its inventor,
Tim Berners-Lee, has his own legitimate claim to be the progenitor of the internet   10
as we know it. The first ever website was his own, at CERN: info.cern.ch.

[...]

Web browsers crossed the border into mainstream use far more rapidly than
had been the case with the internet itself: Mosaic launched in 1993 and Netscape
followed soon after, though it was an embarrassingly long time before Microsoft   15
realised the commercial necessity of getting involved at all. Amazon and eBay were
online by 1995. And in 1998 came Google, offering a powerful new way to search
the proliferating mass of information on the web. [...] Without most of us quite
noticing when it happened, the web went from being a strange new curiosity
to a background condition of everyday life: I have no memory of there being an   20
intermediate stage, when, say, half the information I needed on a particular topic
could be found online, while the other half still required visits to libraries.

From theguardian.com

1 Look at the following statements and decide whether each one applies to Text 1.3,
   Text 1.4 or both. Copy and complete the table, ticking the correct column.
   For each statement, give evidence from the text.

Statement	Text 1.3	Text 1.4	Both	Evidence
The style of the writing is formal.				
The topic is easy to identify.				
The writer communicates directly with the reader.				
Each paragraph starts with a topic sentence indicating what the paragraph is about.				
The writer expresses their thoughts and opinions on the topic.				
The information is clearly presented in a logical order, organised by date.				
The writer uses some features for deliberate impact on the reader.				

2 Read Text 1.3 again and then answer Questions a–d.

   a Give **two** things that were required to access the world wide web, according to paragraph 1.

   b What limited people's use of the world wide web, according to paragraph 1?

   c What led to the commercialisation of the internet, according to paragraph 2?

   d Give **two** facts from paragraph 2 that show how rapidly internet use developed.

Some questions require you to explain a writer's choice of words – either the meanings within the text, or why a particular word or phrase is effective. This is where close reading skills become important.

3 Re-read Text 1.4 and then answer Questions a and b.

   a Use your own words to explain what the text means by:

      i 'easier to navigate' (line 7)   [2]

      ii 'particular topic' (line 21)   [2]

   b Re-read paragraph 2 ('Web browsers . . . libraries').

      i Why does the writer use the word 'curiosity' (line 19) rather than 'invention' to describe the world wide web?   [2]

      ii Explain what the writer suggests about using the internet in the phrase:

        'the proliferating mass of information on the web' (line 18).   [3]

> **TIP**
>
> The command word 'give' asks you to show an explicit understanding of the text. It requires you to select and retrieve information, but not to explain or analyse the text.

> **TIP**
>
> Command words such as 'explain' and 'why', and the instruction to 'use your own words', require you to go further than locating and retrieving information. These commands words mean you need to interpret or analyse the text.

> **REFLECTION**
>
> How confident do you feel about what different command words require you to do?
>
> How confident were you about answering the questions on Texts 1.3 and 1.4?
>
> What areas do you need to improve on?

Text 1.5 is an autobiographical text in which an adult reflects on their childhood. This is a narrative personal account.

> **Text 1.5**
>
> Always a hyperactive kid, I decided to start rock-climbing when I was about four years old. One of my friends held a birthday party at an activity centre with a climbing wall. It was a wall designed for smaller children, so it was pretty tame really, but as soon as I had my harness on, I just went for it and climbed right to the top in minutes. The parents watching just couldn't   5 believe it, as the other kids were really struggling to find the hand- and footholds. It was just instinct for me: I was fearless! From that moment, I knew I just had to climb. My parents decided it would be good to harness my propensity for risk-taking, and they signed me up for a rock-climbing club. I was quickly spotted by someone scouting for the national team, and the rest   10 is history, really.

My parents have consistently supported me – driving me around and even travelling overseas with me. My friends are really great too, although as I've got older, I've found that the majority of my remaining friends are also heavily involved in the sport. I have very little time to do normal teenage socialising, 15 so I suppose it's natural that other friendships have been lost. My brother is the best though, because no matter how many medals and trophies I win, he always treats me as the little sister and still makes me do my share of the washing up! He keeps me fully grounded and stops me from getting conceited and precious about my success. 20

Text 1.6 is a fictional narrative.

Text 1.6

Lifting the window sash, she eased herself up onto the sill and crouched on the ledge for a few seconds. She could hear a noise in the distance, a soft two-note call, probably an owl in pursuit of prey. She held her breath, listening. Kostas had taught her the precise sequence of their hooting: brief note, brief silence, long note, long silence. An owl Morse code just for them. 5

She reached for a limb of the mulberry tree and carefully pulled herself on to it. From there she climbed down, one branch at a time, as she had so often done when she was a little girl. As soon as she jumped to the ground, she looked up to see if anyone had been watching. For a split second she thought she saw a shadow in a window. Could it be her sister? But Meryem should be asleep in her 10 room. She had checked on her earlier.

Her stomach clenching with anxiety, Defne sneaked out of the garden. The moonlight reflected off the stone setts along the narrow streets, forming rivulets of silver that shimmered in front of her as if she were coasting over water. She accelerated her steps, glancing over her shoulder every few seconds to 15 make sure no one was following.

From *The Island of Missing Trees* by Elif Shafak

4   Look at the following statements and decide whether each one applies to Text 1.5, Text 1.6 or both. Copy and complete the table, ticking the correct column. For each statement, give evidence from the text.

Statement	Text 1.5	Text 1.6	Both	Evidence
The text creates suspense and intrigue to hook the reader.				
The text is written in the first person.				
The text communicates thoughts and feelings.				
The text is written as a third-person narrative.				
The text includes personal details about the writer.				
The writer uses some features of descriptive writing to create a setting.				

5 Re-read Text 1.5 and then answer Questions a and b.

a Identify a word or phrase from the text which suggests the same idea as the words in bold ('quite unadventurous' and 'make use of'):

   i The climbing wall was **quite unadventurous** for the writer. [1]

   ii Her parents wanted to **make use of** her bravery. [1]

b Use your own words to explain what the writer means by each of the words in bold:

'My friends are really great too, although as I have got older, I have found that the majority of my remaining friends are also **heavily** involved in the sport. I have **limited** time to do normal teenage socialising, so I suppose it's **natural** that other friendships have been lost.'

   i heavily [1]

   ii limited [1]

   iii natural [1]

Look at the following practice question relating to Text 1.6, then read the two example responses.

Use **one** example from the text below to explain how the writer uses language to suggest that the main character is doing something secretive.

Use your own words in your explanation.

'Lifting the window sash, she eased herself up onto the sill and crouched on the ledge for a few seconds. She could hear a noise in the distance, a soft two-note call, probably an owl in pursuit of prey. She held her breath, listening.' [5]

Answer A

When the writer says she 'eased herself onto the sill and crouched on the ledge', it implies that she is making as little noise as possible. The word 'eased' means moved carefully, which suggests she is avoiding making any sudden movements that could attract attention. The word 'crouched' means she is in a still position where she is hunched and making herself as small as possible. This makes her sound like an animal that is assessing the scene around it, checking that it is safe to move. Overall, her attempts to move without making a noise then staying still in a tight position create the impression that she does not want to be overheard or seen, which is secretive.

Answer B

The writer tells us 'She held her breath, listening'. This shows us that she is very alert to her surroundings, probably because she is doing something secretive and doesn't want to be caught. She may be running away from home and has deliberately left in the dark so people can't see her. It is quite creepy because she can hear 'an owl in pursuit of prey', which is quite scary and like something out of a fairytale. It reminds me of people being lost in the woods and hearing owls which make them jump. Owls are also secretive creatures in lots of stories and very wise.

6 a Which response do you think is more successful? Think about:
   - the instruction in the question to choose 'one example'
   - the number of marks (5)
   - the command words 'Explain how'
   - whether the response considers meanings of words and phrases
   - whether the response considers the effects of the language in terms of how it shapes the reader's understanding.

   b Write your own answer based on the example 'She held her breath, listening' or 'an owl in pursuit of prey'.

7 Use **one** example from the text below to explain how the writer uses language to create atmosphere.

   Use your own words in your explanation.

   'Her stomach clenching with anxiety, Dafne sneaked out of the garden. The moonlight reflected off the stone setts along the narrow streets, forming rivulets of silver that shimmered in front of her as if she were coasting over water. She accelerated her steps, glancing over her shoulder every few seconds to make sure no one was following.'   [5]

REFLECTION

How confident are you about questions using the command words 'Explain how'? What advice would you give to a student about how to select a language example for a 5-mark question?

SELF-ASSESSMENT CHECKLIST

Let's revisit the skills focus for this unit.
Decide how confident you are with each statement.

Now I can	Show it	Needs more work	Almost there	Confident to move on
identify how reading skills are used in everyday life	List five examples of reading you have done today and the text types for each.			
read actively	Write an explanation of active reading.			
understand different reading strategies	Make a list of the different reading strategies you have used in this unit.			
identify the features of different types of fiction and non-fiction texts.	List three differences between fiction and non-fiction texts.			

2 Reading for comprehension

In this unit, you will practise the reading skills necessary to tackle comprehension questions on a previously unseen text. An important part of understanding this kind of question is knowing what command words are and what they mean. This will enable you to interpret the question accurately, to provide a strong answer. Here, you will explore all the command words you might come across, and the reading skills required to respond to them. You will also have opportunities to write answers to exam-style questions.

2.1 Focusing on vocabulary

UNDERSTAND
THESE TERMS

- explicit meaning

- synonym

- nuances

Look at these openings to exam-style questions:

- Identify a word which suggests the same idea as . . .

- Use your own words to explain what the writer means by . . .

In these questions, you are being asked to explain an explicit meaning by identifying or using words with the same meaning as a word or phrase from the original text (synonyms).

In the first type of question ('Identify a word . . .'), you need to locate a specific word in the text that is the same as the idea given in the question. In the second question type ('Use your own words . . .'), you need to remodel the text to explain the writer's meaning in a different way. You can use some words from the source text, but you should reorganise them so that the written expression is your own.

When doing this, it is important to choose the right synonym, because words with similar meanings can have different nuances. For example:

The room was **snug**: warm, inviting and softly lit.

Synonyms for 'snug' include 'cosy', 'comfortable', 'compact' and 'tight', but not all these words would be appropriate, because of their nuances. To show your understanding of the word 'snug', you would need to consider the context in which it is used. The word 'tight' would not work here because it has a negative connotation – that of being uncomfortably small. However, both 'cosy' and 'comfortable' would be appropriate language to describe the room.

《 RECALL AND CONNECT 1 《

What is the definition of a synonym? In pairs, choose a word and then work together to write two synonyms for that word.

---

1   Choose the best synonym from the options in brackets to replace the words in bold ('a fair', 'attentively', 'congratulated', 'challenging', 'exacting', 'genuinely').

She hoped she was **a fair** (an impartial / an honest / a neutral) team leader. She always tried her best to listen **attentively** (scrupulously / deliberately / carefully) when colleagues expressed ideas in meetings, and **congratulated** (saluted / praised / toasted) them for their achievements when they met or exceeded targets. It was more **challenging** (difficult / tough / troublesome) when dealing with those who struggled to meet her rather **exacting** (strict / uncompromising / inflexible) expectations, but she **genuinely** (certainly / authentically / honestly) felt that she led by example, so they had little cause for complaint.

Some comprehension questions require you to explain the meanings of words in the context in which they are used in the text. This means you need to think of a suitable synonym and consider any nuances.

2 Read Text 2.1, then answer the questions.

> **Text 2.1**
>
> Trees generally live much longer than humans and most other living organisms on Earth. Depending on the species, their lifespans can range from under 100 years to several thousand years. One tree species, however, surpasses them all. The Great Basin Bristlecone Pine is recognised as the oldest living tree species, with some individual trees living for more than 5,000 years.   5
>
> The Great Basin Bristlecone Pine's extraordinary longevity is largely due to the extreme environment in which it grows. Harsh conditions such as freezing temperatures, strong winds, and an extremely slow growth rate result in very dense wood. In some years, growth is so minimal that no   10 new growth rings form. This dense wood and slow growth make the tree highly resistant to insects, fungi, decay, and erosion. Additionally, the sparse vegetation in its habitat means Great Basin Bristlecone Pines are rarely affected by wildfires. Despite their slow growth, these trees can reach heights of up to 50 feet and develop trunks with diameters as large as 154 inches.   15

a Use your own words to explain what the text means by:

    i 'lifespans can range' (line 2)   [2]

    ii 'recognised as the oldest' (lines 4–5)   [2]

    iii 'Harsh conditions' (line 8)   [2]

    iv 'highly resistant' (line 12)   [2]

You may also be asked to explain why a writer has chosen to use a particular word instead of another word with a similar meaning. For this, you need to consider the nuances of each word and explain the subtle differences in meaning. For example:

> After the long wedding ceremony was finally over, the guests **devoured** the buffet.

Here, the writer has used the word 'devoured' rather than 'ate' because it makes it clear that they were eating very quickly and were very hungry.

3 Explain why the writer uses the words 'gobbled', 'browsed' and 'demolished' rather than 'ate' in the following sentences.

  a When the boring wedding ceremony was finally over, the guests **gobbled** the buffet.

  b When the elegant wedding ceremony was finally over, the guests **browsed** the buffet.

  c When the late wedding ceremony was finally over, the guests **demolished** the buffet.

2.2 Putting reading strategies into practice

Before you start writing an answer, make sure you have fully understood the question. Look carefully at the command word, as well as any other key words, as these will tell you how to frame your response. You can use your skim reading skills to find important information in the question.

'Give', 'what' and 'find' are usually asking you to select explicit information from the text. You do not need to use your own words in the answer, but you should be selective in the information you include in your response.

'Explain', 'assess' and 'justify' require you to show more implicit understanding, by making judgements or analysing the information in the text.

You should also pay attention to how many marks each question is worth, in order to plan your time effectively.

1   Read Text 2.2, then read the comprehension questions in Activity 2 below.

   a   Look at each command word. For each question, are you being asked to find or retrieve explicit information, explore implicit meanings, or both?

   b   Would you need to use the reading strategy of skim reading or scanning to answer each question?

   c   Which questions require you to use your own words in the response?

   d   Look at the marks allocated for each question. How many points do you think you need to include in your response?

   e   How long do you think you should spend answering each question?

UNDERSTAND THESE TERMS

- command word
- implicit meaning

TIP

Remember that comprehension questions usually follow the order of the text, so you can move through the text, skim reading and scanning for the answers.

Text 2.2

Megacities are defined as urban areas where more than 10 million people live. A large proportion of the population live in high-rise buildings in a densely packed environment with no outdoor space and high levels of noise pollution. Most megacities expand rapidly, and as they spread outwards, it becomes increasingly challenging to provide   5
efficient services and transport.

Vast numbers of people move to megacities from the countryside, attracted by the promise of job opportunities. In many countries, rural areas are now experiencing declining opportunities due to a lack of investment, so young people flock to the cities in search of a better life.   10
As a result, the last few decades have witnessed an enormous cultural shift, and urban life has come to represent progress and modernity due to superior technology and connectivity.

However, rapid mass migration into cities brings problems too, as they struggle to provide enough basic resources to cope with the population   15
explosion. This often leads to power outages and water shortages. If large numbers of the rural poor migrate to the cities, affordable housing becomes scarce, and unofficial settlements (often known as slums) spring up. Here, poor sanitation increases health risks for the people living there.   20

Megacities also usually suffer from poor air quality, due to construction and heavy transportation. As the cities expand outwards in an urban sprawl, green spaces and wildlife habitats are lost. Public transport systems cannot keep up with demand and become crowded and unreliable. This leads to higher private car ownership – and, inevitably, an increase in traffic congestion. Further road expansions simply exacerbate rather than solve the issue.   25

Experts have projected that by 2030, almost 60% of the world's population will live in urban areas, and a high proportion of these will reside in megacities. Significant wealth inequality in cities will lead to   30
a widening divide between rich and poor in the coming years, due to increasing housing costs and educational inequality, limiting social mobility. Rural population decline could lead to agricultural labour shortages and farming becoming less economically viable. Ageing rural populations may become increasingly isolated as the more   35
educated and skilled younger generations flock to higher-paid jobs in the cities, weakening family support systems leading to a loss of community cohesion.

2   Answer the questions about Text 2.2.

   a   What kind of homes do most people live in when they reside
       in megacities, according to paragraph 1?   [1]

   b   Use your own words to explain what the text means by:

       i   'expand rapidly' (line 4)   [2]

       ii   'declining opportunities' (line 9)   [2]

   c   Re-read Paragraph 2 ('Vast numbers . . . technology and connectivity').
       Give **two** reasons for the movement of people from rural areas
       to megacities.   [2]

   d   Re-read paragraph 3 ('However, . . . for the people living there.').
       Identify the **two** main reasons for the difficulties providing basic
       resources in megacities.   [2]

REFLECTION

What did you find challenging about answering these comprehension questions? Are there any areas you need to improve upon? If so, how will you go about that?

2.3 Using your own words

Questions that ask you to respond using your own words might be assessing your understanding of words and phrases in the context in which they are used in the text, or they may be assessing your understanding of implicit meaning. When answering these questions, it is important not to copy from the text – you need to paraphrase effectively, without changing the original meaning.

1   Rewrite the following sentences, using your own words as far as possible.

   a   All young people need to be cautious when using social media to avoid falling prey to its many pitfalls and pressures.

   b   Achieving fluency in a foreign language is something we should all aspire to, regardless of our native tongue.

   c   Being an older sibling instils many virtues in a child, including responsibility, maturity and good judgement.

   d   The dark, antique furniture made the house look depressing – as if it was stuck in the past.

   e   The exam hall was brightly lit, with the rows of small, single, wooden desks reminding students that their future was in their own hands and no one else's.

A comprehension question may ask you to look for a word or phrase in the text that has a similar meaning to one in bold in the question. For this, you need to use your skills of skimming and scanning to quickly locate a similar idea from the clues in the question sentence.

2   Identify a word or a phrase from Text 2.2 which suggests the same idea as the words in bold ('improved chance of finding work', 'development and the contemporary lifestyle', 'growing shortage of cheap accommodation', 'made predictions', 'prevent people from improving their living standards'):

   a   Many individuals relocate to cities due to **an improved chance of finding work** when they get there.   [1]

   b   For many people, living in a city symbolises **development and the contemporary lifestyle** that they desire.   [1]

   c   Some people end up homeless due to a **growing shortage of cheap accommodation**.   [1]

   d   Experts have **made predictions** that in the future, more people will live in cities than in the countryside.   [1]

   e   Unfair access to school could **prevent people from improving their living standards** in the future.   [1]

You may also be asked to explain what the writer means by particular words in the text. The words usually come from the same paragraph and vary in difficulty – some of them may be used in a figurative or non-literal way. For these questions, it is important to read the whole paragraph rather than just looking at the words in isolation, which is why the whole paragraph is given to you in the question.

UNDERSTAND THIS TERM

- paraphrase

TIP

Remember – the command word 'explain' means that you need to use your own words to show full understanding of the text.

TIP

It is fine to use a few individual words from the original text. Just make sure that you remodel the language enough for it to be accepted as your own words.

3   Use your own words to explain what the writer means by each of the words in bold:

'Rural population decline could lead to agricultural **labour** shortages and farming becoming less economically viable. Ageing rural populations may become increasingly **isolated** as the more educated and skilled younger generations **flock** to higher-paid jobs in the cities, weakening family support systems leading to a loss of community cohesion.'

a   labour   [1]

b   isolated   [1]

c   flock   [1]

TIP

The meaning you give in response to questions like this must fit with the context, so nuances matter. Look for clues in the text if you are unsure of a word's meaning. Remember that you can use more than one word in your explanation if you need to.

REFLECTION

What are the challenges of explaining the meanings of words within the context of a text? What can you do to meet these challenges? Make a list of tips to help you remember the key learning points. For example, 'Avoid using very similar words in the explanation'.

2.4 Explicit and implicit meaning

Comprehension questions are designed to assess your understanding of both explicit and implicit meanings of a reading text. So far in this unit, you have mostly practised identifying the explicit meaning of words in context and retrieved explicit information. However, you will also have to infer a writer's meaning by looking more closely at what the writer implies. Questions that require an understanding of implicit meaning often have more marks allocated to them because your explanations need to be more developed.

<< RECALL AND CONNECT 2 <<

Different questions will test your understanding of explicit and implicit meaning and your skills of inference. What is the difference between explicit and implicit meaning? What is the difference between implying and inferring?

1   Answer the following questions based on Text 2.2.

Re-read paragraphs 4 and 5 ('Megacities also . . . community cohesion').

a   Explain why traffic congestion becomes a problem as megacities develop.   [3]

b   Explain how the rise of megacities will lower the quality of life for those left in rural areas.   [3]

Sometimes, you will have to explain why a writer uses a particular word. These questions want you to explore the implications of the writer's vocabulary choice, to assess your implicit understanding of the text. You need to explain why the chosen word is more effective or powerful than the alternative word given in the question.

TIP

In a 3-mark comprehension question, 1 or 2 marks will be based on explicit understanding through explaining meaning or retrieving information. However, to access all 3 marks, you will also need to show understanding of implicit meaning.

2 Look at this task and the sample responses.

> Why does the writer use the word 'roaring' rather than the word 'loud' to describe the wind?

Answer A

The writer uses the word 'roaring' to make the wind sound louder than it is. The word 'loud' also tells us that it is 'loud' but not as much as 'roaring'.

Answer B

The writer uses the word 'roaring' to exaggerate the sound of the wind and make it sound threatening, because 'roaring' has associations with being fierce and dangerous. The word 'loud' does not have the same dramatic effect, as it is simply factual, so it has no emotional impact on the reader.

Compare the two answers. Which one is more successful? Why? What feedback would you give to each of the students?

Similar questions may focus on a writer's use of a particular phrase, often involving figurative language. You will need to provide a full explanation in your response, with three clear points.

3 Look at this task, and the sample responses.

> Explain what the writer suggests about the storm in the phrase:
>
> 'it raged throughout the night, violently thrashing its branches against the windows'.

Answer A

The word 'raged' makes the storm sound angry, as if deliberately trying to cause harm. This is developed by the word 'thrashing' and the implication that the storm is using the branches of the trees to aggressively hit the windows of the house as if intentionally trying to cause destruction. As a whole, the storm is described as a living being with sinister intentions.

Answer B

The storm is made to sound very violent and frightening like a person in a rage. The trees are thrashing against the windows which must make a very loud sound and be frightening. It paints a very vivid picture of the storm in the reader's mind.

Compare the two answers. Which one is more successful? Why? What feedback would you give to each of the students?

TIP

When answering questions explaining a writer's word choices, remember to think about nuance, connotations, figurative language and how powerful a word is.

TIP

In this type of question, make sure you comment on both words, not just the word used by the writer, to ensure that you consider the contrasting impact of the words.

4 Read Text 2.3 and then answer Questions a–d.

> **Text 2.3**
>
> The Vjosa River in Albania has been proclaimed the last 'wild river' outside
> Russia – which simply means that it is a river that flows from its source
> to the sea without humans attempting to tame its flow. Instead, it braids
> itself through diverse landscapes, meandering in multiple directions on
> its 272-kilometre journey from the Pindus Mountains to the Adriatic Sea.   5
> The river's untouched beauty and pristine turquoise waters as it weaves its
> way through charming little towns are testament to its wild splendour.
>
> In 2023, after a decade-long campaign by environmental organisations, the
> Vjosa was declared the first wild river national park in Europe – a historic
> decision that puts Albania as a leader in river protection, offering a model   10
> of conservation. The rest of the European continent has the most obstructed
> river landscape on Earth, with over a million constructions such as dams,
> embankments and fjords affecting biodiversity, as well as destroying the
> naturally rich beauty of river landscapes.
>
> Whether you are a hiker, birdwatcher, water sports lover or a nature   15
> enthusiast, the Vjosa will welcome you with open arms and endless
> possibilities for adventure.

a Why does the writer use the words 'proclaimed' (line 1) rather than
word 'called' to refer to the Vjosa's recognition as a wild river? [2]

b Explain what the writer suggests about the river in the phrase:

'braids itself through diverse landscapes, meandering in multiple
directions' (lines 3–4). [3]

c Why does the writer use the word 'historic' (line 9) instead of the
word 'significant' to describe the decision to declare the Vjosa River
a national park? [2]

d Explain what the writer suggests about the decision to declare the
River Vjosa a national park in the phrase:

'puts Albania as a leader in river protection offering a model of
conservation' (lines 10–11). [3]

SELF-ASSESSMENT CHECKLIST

Let's revisit the skills focus for this unit.

Now I can	Show it	Needs more work	Almost there	Confident to move on
use different strategies to build vocabulary through reading	Make a list of the new vocabulary you have learnt during this unit.			
understand how to respond to a variety of comprehension questions	List six command words and explain whether each one requires information retrieval, explicit or implicit meanings or a developed explanation to show implicit understanding.			
select appropriate information from texts for different purposes	Explain what reading strategy needs to be used for selecting appropriate information from texts and why.			
explain meanings in texts in my own words	Choose the opening sentence of three of the texts in this chapter and rewrite each one in your own words.			
identify explicit and implicit meanings in a variety of texts.	Write a sentence about your favourite food where the meaning is explicit. Now write another sentence about it where the meaning is implied.			

Exam practice 1

The questions in this section will allow you to demonstrate the skills you have covered in Units 1 and 2 and will help you prepare for your assessment.

The following text and questions have example student responses and commentaries. Write your own responses to the questions first, then compare your responses to the examples. Read the commentaries carefully and see whether any of the comments apply to your response, then revise your responses to improve them.

Read Text A and then answer **Questions 1a–f** and **2a–b**.

Text A

Murano is one of the small islands situated in the Venice Lagoon and accessible by a public water bus, which takes 15 minutes. It is world-renowned for its glass production, which started in 1291, when the glassmakers of Venice were ordered by the authorities to relocate their furnaces to Murano. This was due to the danger of fire destroying the city's mostly wooden buildings and bridges. 5

Murano's glassmakers (or 'maestros' as they were known) became the island's most important citizens. In the 14th century, they were immune from prosecution to illustrate their wealth and privilege. However, they were also forbidden to leave the region in order to protect the glass industry and stop them from taking their knowledge and skills to mainland Europe. 10

Many technologies still associated with glassmaking were historically developed on Murano, including enamelled glass, glass infused with gold threads, multicoloured glass and imitation gemstones made of glass. Their crafting methods were kept secret for centuries, and today many of the most famous glass brands in the world still own factories in Murano. All glass made there has a trademark to certify its 15 origin as Murano glass.

Today, large numbers of tourists flock to the glass factories on Murano, which are now open to the public. They can observe skilled glassmakers using many centuries-old techniques to craft items. Glassblowing workshops are available, where – for an extra fee – tourists can watch a 'glass maestro' create a vase or 20 one of the animal figurines the island is still famous for. Visitors usually exit the building through the souvenir shop associated with the factory visit, where they are encouraged to purchase their own glassware to take home.

Unfortunately, the surging availability of cheap air travel in recent decades has left destinations such as Murano facing the problem of over-tourism, which has 25 devastating impacts on local communities. More properties are rented out using online platforms, meaning that there are more tourists than locals on the island at the busiest times of the year. This drives up housing costs and forces the younger generations to leave the area. Locals also complain that the swarms of excited visitors descending from cruise ships day after day significantly erode their quality of life. 30

Question 1

a   What is Murano famous for, according to paragraph 1?   [1]

Example student response	Examiner comments
It is world-renowned for its glass production, which started in 1291 when the glassmakers of Venice were ordered by the authorities to relocate their furnaces to Murano.	This response needs to be more selective, rather than copying a whole sentence from paragraph 1. The simpler 'its glass production' would demonstrate a more secure understanding of the question and the text. 0/1 mark

b   Use your own words to explain what the text means by:

   i   'ordered by the authorities' (lines 3–4)   [2]

Example student response	Examiner comments
Instructed by the authorities.	This response is partially correct, as the word 'ordered' has been explained. However, the student has not explained the meaning of 'the authorities' but has simply lifted the word from the text/question. The responses should have stated 'ordered by the government' or 'those in charge' in order to gain full marks. 1/2 marks

   ii   'due to the danger' (lines 4–5)   [2]

Example student response	Examiner comments
Because of the risk posed.	This is a good response, which explains 'due to' as 'because of' and 'danger' as 'risk posed'. The whole phrase has been explained, so it would achieve both available marks. 2/2 marks

c   Re-read paragraph 2 ('Murano's glassmakers . . . Europe').
   Give **one** advantage and **one** disadvantage of being a glass maestro in
   Murano, due to their important status.   [2]

Example student response	Examiner comments
One advantage is that the glassmakers were protected from being prosecuted. The other advantage is that they were wealthy.	This response is only partially successful. Although the student has identified an advantage correctly (that they were protected from being prosecuted), they have not read the question carefully enough, so no disadvantage is identified. Instead, they have made a general observation that they were wealthy and offered it incorrectly as a second advantage. The disadvantage needed for full marks is that they were forbidden to leave the area. 1/2 marks

d   Re-read paragraph 3 ('Many technologies . . . Murano glass').
    Identify **two** reasons why Murano glass is still considered desirable today.   [2]

Example student response	Examiner comments
The glass is still desirable today because it is made using traditional crafting methods and it carries a trademark to show it was made there so is special.	This response would get full marks, as the student has correctly identified two reasons why Murano glass is still considered desirable. 2/2 marks

e   Re-read paragraph 4 ('Today, . . . take home.')

   i   Explain how the glass industry has adapted its ways to maximise profit
       from tourism.   [3]

Example student response	Examiner comments
Workers in the glass industry are no longer expected to work in secret, and the industry holds special events for tourists, such as watching the glassmakers at work. They have shops attached to the factories in which tourists can buy glass objects to take home.	This response is partially effective, as it offers two ways in which the industry has adapted to tourism (the special events and the shops). However, this is a 3-mark question, so a response should make three distinct points. The third idea needed is that the factories are now open to the public. 2/3 marks

   ii   Explain why some tourists may not enjoy a visit to a glass factory
        on Murano.   [3]

Example student response	Examiner comments
Some tourists may not enjoy the crowds in the glass factories. They also may not like the fact that you have to pay extra fees for some activities. Having to exit through the souvenir shop adds pressure to buy things and some tourists may not enjoy that as they end up spending too much.	This is a good answer, in which the student has correctly inferred that the factories are likely to be overcrowded and put pressure on tourists to spend money on extra displays as well as forcing them to go through the shop as they leave to tempt them into buying gifts. Three distinct ideas are offered, showing understanding of implicit meaning. 3/3 marks

f Re-read paragraph 5 ('Unfortunately, . . . quality of life').

    i Why does the writer use the word 'surging' (line 24) rather than 'growing' to describe the availability of cheap air travel? [2]

Example student response	Examiner comments
The word 'surging' makes it sound as if the growth of cheap air travel is happening too fast. It makes it sound uncontrolled.	The word 'surging' is explained well here. However, the students should also consider why the word 'growing' does not have the same impact to offer a full response. They should have added that growing does not have the same impact as it does not capture the idea of speed in the same way. 1/2 marks

    ii Explain what the writer suggests about the impact of tourism in the phrase: 'the swarms of excited visitors descending from cruise ships day after day' (lines 29–30). [3]

Example student response	Examiner comments
This phrase makes the tourists sound like insects swarming all over the place. It makes them sound really dangerous as if they might hurt people so it makes the place sound frightening and hostile to be in.	The student makes a link between the word 'swarming' and insects but interprets the effect of this as indicating danger. This is not very convincing in the context of this text, where 'swarming' is used to emphasise the numbers of tourists and how unpleasantly crowded it makes the place. The student has also not considered the whole phrase and the implications of 'day after day' so the response is not as developed as it should be for a 3-mark question. 1/3 marks

Question 2

a Identify a word or phrase from the text which suggests the same idea as the words in bold ('hundreds of years' and 'crowds of visitors go'):

    i Their ways of making glass objects were kept hidden in Murano for **hundreds of years**. [1]

Example student response	Examiner comments
In the past.	This response is incorrect, as 'in the past' does not have the same meaning as 'hundreds of years'. Also, the phrase does not fit grammatically into the sentence in the question. 'Centuries' is the correct answer. 0/1 marks

ii   Nowadays, **crowds of visitors go** to visit the glass factories on Murano.   [1]

Example student response	Examiner comments
large numbers of tourists flock	This response reflects and quotes the correct phrase from the text to replace the phrase in bold. 1/1 mark

b   Use your own words to explain what the writer means by each of the words in bold:

'In the 14th century they were immune from prosecution to **illustrate** their wealth and importance. However, they were also **forbidden** to leave the **region** in order to protect the glass industry and stop them from taking their knowledge and skills to mainland Europe.'

i   illustrate   [1]

Example student response	Examiner comments
show	This response is correct. 1/1 mark

ii   forbidden   [1]

Example student response	Examiner comments
Allowed	This response is incorrect, as it does not explain the meaning of 'forbidden'. A better answer would have been 'not allowed' or 'banned'. 0/1 marks

iii   region   [1]

Example student response	Examiner comments
area	This response is correct. 1/1 mark

3 Summary writing

In this unit, you will practise planning and writing summaries based on unseen texts. Planning is a key part of writing a successful summary, so first you will look carefully at the question to make sure you understand what is required. You will then consider how to plan effectively so you can organise your ideas logically, as well as exploring how to use language appropriately to write a fluent response within the 120-word limit.

In addition to writing a summary in the exam, you will have to complete another task based on the same text. So, in this unit you will also practise assessing the writer's attitude towards an aspect of the topic covered in an unseen text.

3.1 Reading for ideas

When writing a summary, you are creating a shortened version of the source text by focusing on the specific areas of the content that are outlined in the question. It is therefore important to read the question carefully to identify the main points you need to include. To begin with, you need to recognise whether a question has one or two strands to address. This informs the points you select from the text and how you organise your response.

To respond effectively to a summary question, you need to:

1   Skim read the text to form an overview of the main idea.

2   Read the question carefully, noting how many strands it has.

3   Scan the text, looking for the main content points to address the focus of the question, then record them in brief bullet points.

4   Review your bullet points and synthesise similar ones. Cross out any repeated points.

5   Consider the question focus and reorder the points to organise the response logically.

6   Use your plan to write up your summary, in your own words, as far as possible.

7   Check your summary to ensure you have used a neutral tone and written fluently.

1   Decide whether the following exam-style questions have one or two strands.

a   According to the text, what are the main causes of global warming and what can countries do to prevent them?

b   According to the text, what flood defence measures can be implemented quickly to stop further devastation?

c   According to the text, what are the benefits of elephants living in captivity rather than in the wild?

d   According to the text, what are the advantages and disadvantages of buying an eco-friendly property to live in?

To begin a summary response, you should skim read the text to form an overview of what it is about. It helps to think in terms of the writer's purpose and audience.

2   Skim read Texts 3.1 and 3.2, then write a one- or two-sentence overview of each one.

Text 3.1

Living a healthy lifestyle with plenty of exercise is undoubtedly good for long-term health. However, recent research suggests that the current trend of taking up long-distance running with the sole purpose of completing a marathon could lead to risk of serious injuries. Very few people stop to consider their current state of physical health when deciding to run a marathon with a group of friends, or to support a charitable cause. As a result, many do not prepare properly for the big day and end up full of

5

disappointment when their race is cut short because of a hamstring injury –
or worse. Unless a programme of training is planned carefully and followed
rigorously, it's highly unlikely that a couch potato is going to transform into   10
a marathon runner by doing a few 10-kilometre runs in the months leading
up to the event. Taking care of your body through a nutritious diet, careful
hydration, and buying the right equipment is essential as a starting point.

Text 3.2

Nomadic communities are made up of people in remote areas who
live in temporary homes and travel from place to place. They have the
knowledge and ability to sustain their lives by finding food, grazing their
livestock or finding work wherever they go. They often move according
to the seasons, so have a fixed pattern over each year.   5

As societies have changed and become more dependent on modern
devices and technology, the vast majority of people around the globe
choose to live in permanent residences, and there are fewer and
fewer nomadic communities. However, a number have survived and
persist with this traditional way of life despite the presence of modern   10
amenities. One example is the Bedouin people, who have historically
inhabited desert regions in the Middle East and North Africa, living in
tents. Another is the Maasai of Kenya and Tanzania, where some tribes
still raise livestock in areas including the Rift Valley and the Serengeti.
In Mongolia, there are still nomadic communities that live in traditional   15
yurts and move up to ten times a year. All these groups have a unique
knowledge of the ecosystem and biodiversity of their countries due to
a deep understanding of the landscapes they inhabit, which has been
passed down through the generations.

However, there are many threats to these dwindling nomadic   20
communities, including climate change, which leads to extreme weather
patterns that bring both droughts and intense rainfall. Adventure
tourism also has a detrimental effect in more remote areas, encroaching
upon the territories of nomadic people, invading their privacy and
making them the object of curiosity. Some governments have   25
introduced policies to restrict the movements of nomadic communities
as a result of discriminatory attitudes towards those who choose to live
life differently from the norm.

Once you have the gist of the text and have interrogated the question to determine
what main points to include, you need to read the text again more closely to identify
these points. Remember – you should only include essential information in a summary.
You do not need supporting details or examples in a summary.

A supporting detail is additional information that a writer uses to illustrate a point.
For example, in a summary about the problems caused by changes in migratory
behaviour, a main point could be that the issue affects local ecosystems with the details
that there is less insect consumption and seed pollination. You would only need to
include the main point, as the details are excess information.

Writers use examples to show what a main point means. For instance, the main point could be that, as a result of changes in migratory behaviour, some species are declining in number; examples here might be numbers of specific species, such as the nightingale and cuckoo. Again, you would only need to include the main point in a summary, not the examples.

3 Look at the following task and the list of notes that form part of a plan for an example response.

> According to Text 3.2, what are the characteristics of nomadic communities and what threatens their way of life?

Characteristics of nomadic communities:

- They come from remote areas.
- They travel to different places.
- They have no permanent homes.
- The Bedouin live in the desert.
- They have their own livestock.
- The Maasai live in Kenya and Tanzania.
- Mongolian nomads live in yurts.
- They live traditionally.
- They understand the ecosystem of their region.
- They pass knowledge down through generations.

Threats to their way of life:

- Climate change
- Societies changing
- Modern facilities/equipment
- Wanting to live in permanent homes
- Extreme weather patterns
- Drought and heavy rain
- Increasing tourism in remote areas
- Government policies
- Discrimination.

Copy the list of notes and then complete the following tasks.

a Decide which points from the list are main ideas. Mark them with an asterisk.

b Decide which points are supporting details or examples and cross them out.

c Identify any repetition and cross it out.

TIP

Occasionally, a main idea may only be expressed through examples. In these cases, you will need to rephrase the example as a main point in a concise way and using your own words. For example, a text could state: 'Another threat to human health in urban areas is stationary cars and other vehicles emitting fumes on streets where children are walking to school.' You could summarise this using the words 'another threat is pollution caused by traffic jams'.

Once you are confident that your plan only contains main points, check it again to identify whether any of those points are very similar or connected to each other. If so, they can be synthesised – combined into one sentence – to ensure you keep your summary concise.

Then the final step in the planning process is to reorder the points into a logical order – a sequence that makes sense and is easy for the reader to follow. The summary should flow clearly from one idea to the next, so you might want to follow the order of information in the original text, or it might be more logical to group related ideas.

4   Go back to the list you created in Activity 3.

   a   Look for any similar points that could be synthesised to make the summary more cohesive.

   b   Number the points in the final list to decide on the order in which they should appear.

5   Read the text again, then answer the question.

According to Text 3.2, what are the characteristics of nomadic communities and what threatens their way of life?

Use continuous writing (not note form) and use your own words as far as possible.

Your summary should not be more than 120 words.

Up to 10 marks are available for reading and up to 5 marks for writing.   [15]

Now think about a 'writer's attitude' question based on Text 3.2. The command word 'assess' means to make an informed judgement. So, when you are asked to assess the writer's attitude, you need to clearly identify attitudes and then use examples from the text to support your ideas. This evidence can be examples or brief quotations.

> **RECALL AND CONNECT 1** <<

Explain what you need to do if you are asked to find a detail in a text. Think about whether or not you should answer in your own words and whether evidence is needed.

6   Read Text 3.2 again. As you read, think about the writer's attitude towards nomadic communities. Then look at the three attitudes below. Find a brief quotation in the text to support each one.

   a   admiring of their abilities/knowledge

   b   respectful of their culture

   c   concerned about their survival.

7   Assess the writer's attitude towards nomadic communities.

Use **three** details from Text 3.2 to support your answer.   [5]

8   Read Text 3.3, an article about learning through play. Look at the task, then answer the questions.

   According to Text 3.3, in what ways do young children benefit from play and what can adults do to maximise the benefits?

> **TIP**
>
> It is important to develop the right vocabulary to define attitudes. Think about positive attitudes such as enthusiasm, excitement, passion, determination and admiration and commitment. Also think of more negative attitudes such as shock, concern, frustration and anger. There are some less intense attitudes, too, such as intrigue, scepticism and doubt.

Text 3.3

We all remember games we loved to play when we were children, but are you aware that for children in the early years of their lives, playing is crucial for development as human beings? In most cultures, play is recognised as a child's right – and as a result, early-years education focuses on using play to allow children to make sense of the world around them and to develop important social skills. So, it may look like play, but it is actually a child's work!   5

Play appeals to a child's innate sense of curiosity and desire to explore, particularly when they are free to choose their activity rather than given direct instructions, such as using flashcards to learn new words. In addition,   10
whether through painting and drawing, banging on a drum, listening to stories or singing songs with actions, a child's imagination is stimulated through creative play. Play also teaches children about important social rules, such as taking turns and collaborating with others, as well as developing crucial physical skills.   15

However, research suggests that play needs specific qualities to be truly educational. For example, it needs to actively engage children rather than focus on passive involvement. Constructive play does not need to rely on any predetermined goals or outcomes. Indeed, play should rely on spontaneity, and an element of choice is desirable so children can choose   20
their activity rather than be forced into doing something that doesn't appeal to them at that moment. This forms a clear distinction between the adult concept of work and children's play: adult work is directed by specific goals and outcomes, whereas children's play is centred around enjoyment and exploration. Research suggests that play is most beneficial when there is   25
some adult guidance rather than being left entirely to their own devices, but it needs to be subtle enough not to remove the child's sense of autonomy and self-direction.

According to neuroscience research, the first six years of a child's life form the basis for learning, behaviour and health for the whole of their life. This   30
is due to the influences on the neural pathways in the brain of thinking, exploration, problem solving and use of language, which are stimulated through periods of play, improving academic performance later in life. Indeed, according to the Canadian Council on Learning, 'Play nourishes every aspect of children's development – it forms the foundation of   35
intellectual, social, and physical skills as well as the emotional awareness necessary for success in school and life. Play paves the way for learning'.

a   How many strands does this question have? Identify the focus areas for a plan for this task.

b   Make a bulleted list of the main points, avoiding details and examples.

c   Reorganise the points so they appear in a logical order and synthesise any similar ideas.

TIP

Remember – when identifying points that could be synthesised, think about whether they are saying something so similar that you can fuse the ideas. For example, the idea that children should be actively engaged in play is very close to the idea that they should enjoy it. You could link those ideas by saying: 'Play should be both engaging and enjoyable.'

9 **a** According to Text 3.3, in what ways do young children benefit from play and what can adults do to maximise the benefits?

Use continuous writing (not note form) and use your own words, as far as possible.

Your summary should not be more than 120 words.

Up to 10 marks are available for reading and up to 5 marks for writing.   [15]

b Assess the writer's attitude towards how children should play.

Use **three** details from Text 3.3 to support your answer.   [5]

3.2 Remodelling the text

Planning a summary by identifying, reorganising and synthesising the points is the first step. Next, you need to think about the best ways of writing your summary to present a clear and coherent response to the question.

When writing a summary, use a formal style and a neutral tone. You can achieve this by removing any persuasive or figurative language. For example, if the original text was part of a travel guide persuading people to visit a tourist spot, and the task asked you what visitors would find to do there, your response would be a more factual and informative account than the original text.

≪ RECALL AND CONNECT 2 ≪

What does 'nuance' mean? Why is it important to consider the nuances of words when you paraphrase or remodel a text?

1 Remodel each of these phrases from Text 3.3, using your own words as far as possible.

a allow children to make sense of the world around them

b a child's imagination is stimulated through creative play

c the child's sense of autonomy and self-direction

d some adult guidance

e improving academic performance later in life

2 Which of the following are conventions of formal writing?

- the passive voice
- direct speech
- colloquial expressions
- not using contractions
- reported speech
- slang
- sophisticated language
- a serious tone.

UNDERSTAND THESE TERMS

- formality
- tone
- register
- conventions
- passive voice
- direct speech
- reported speech

TIP

When writing a summary, you are not expected to find synonyms for every word – key words do not need to be changed. However, you should avoid copying whole phrases and sentences.

3 Look at this example summary response to the task below, about an unseen text. Rewrite the paragraph using more neutral, formal language and to reduce the word count to about 120 words (it is currently 240 words).

> According to the text, what experiences and facilities does Nairobi National Park offer visitors?

There is so much going on in Nairobi National Park, it's amazing. It's the most fantastic area of wilderness where we went on a game drive with a guide who knew everything and saw massive herds of zebra and literally hundreds of buffaloes grazing! They also have masses of lions roaming around (which might be a bit scary for some visitors) as well as over 80 rhinos. We were driven miles to the hippo pool too and watched them standing in the water and snoozing in the sun. Watch out though as there are crocodiles lurking in the water too. We couldn't believe that such a massive national park is right on the edge of the city so it couldn't be easier to get there for the day. There are brilliant places to stay as well like Emakoko Lodge or the Nairobi tented camp which is inside the park itself. Prepare yourself though because it means you can listen to the sounds of animals roaring and fighting when you're trying to get a bit of sleep and wake up to the sounds of the birds at dawn. The birds are phenomenal: we saw ostriches and cranes really close up – totally awesome. If you are doing a day trip, the picnic sites are awesome places to enjoy the scenery and wildlife. Pick up a map at the visitor centre and have a look at the educational exhibits while you're there too.

3.3 Developing a coherent summary

Once you have planned your summary and considered how to write it in a neutral, formal tone, you need to think about how to organise the information. To achieve a fluent and coherent summary, you must:

- organise and structure your ideas
- use a range of sentence structures, appropriate vocabulary and suitable connectives to link the ideas.

Using a variety of sentence structures will help the fluency of your writing. You can achieve this by using coordinating conjunctions to link similar points together in one sentence, or by using subordinate clauses to organise the information effectively. Using relative pronouns and present participles will also enable you to vary sentence types and present information logically and fluently.

You should also use connectives such as 'moreover', 'furthermore', 'finally', 'however' and 'nevertheless' to link separate sentences fluently and to signal the development of ideas. However, you should not use too many connectives, so choose them carefully.

> **TIP**
>
> A summary should be one or two paragraphs, and you should always aim to keep within the 120-word limit. A few words more or less will not matter, but a summary that is significantly longer than the specified word count is likely to include unnecessary material, and a summary that is significantly shorter may lack range in the reading ideas you have chosen.

> **UNDERSTAND THESE TERMS**
>
> - coordinating conjunction
> - subordinate clause
> - relative pronouns
> - present participles

> **TIP**
>
> Even if there are two strands in a summary question, it is still fine to only write one paragraph for your response, as long as you respond to both strands in that paragraph.

1 Combine each of the examples below into a single sentence using one of the following coordinating conjunctions:

so   **but**   **yet**

 a In Canada, temperatures plummet during the winter. People still spend a lot of time enjoying outdoor leisure pursuits.

 b Public transport workers went on strike last week. Many people opted to cycle through the city to get to work.

 c They were hoping to visit the park. It was raining heavily outside.

2 Combine each of the examples below into a single sentence, using one of the following relative pronouns:

who   **which**   **when**

 a The lead actress won an award for her performance in the film. She gave a speech thanking the rest of the cast and crew for their support.

 b The truck is parked in the loading bay. It is full of brand-new office furniture.

 c The car went rolling down the hill. Its handbrake failed.

3 Combine the sentences in the examples below by using present participles (words ending in '-ing' formed from a verb). You will need to change the word order.

 a The herd stopped and listened intently. They sensed the presence of a predator.

 b The heron hovered over the pond. It had spotted the fish below.

 c The family ran excitedly to the café. They hoped that the cakes had not sold out.

4 Look at the following example of a summary response to the task below. Rewrite this example, improving the fluency and reorganising the ideas so they are presented more effectively. You can change the order, vocabulary and punctuation. You should also try to reduce it to 120 words (it is currently 150 words).

> According to the text, what are the most interesting and significant features of the Great Wall of China?

The Great Wall of China is 21,196 kilometres long. It took more than 2000 years to construct. It is a popular tourist attraction. It is the largest human-made structure in the world. It stretches across 15 northern Chinese regions. There are 15 passes along the route that have geographical importance. It was built as a series of fortifications. It was designed to be a fortified defence system. More than 10 million people visit the Great Wall of China every year. It is built from lots of different materials. Some of the materials used are bricks, stone blocks and wood. Workers building the wall left marks on the bricks. Some more remote sections of the wall are crumbling. It is one of the most famous landmarks in the world. The Badaling section of the wall near Beijing is the most commonly visited by tourists. Some parts of the wall are very steep and considered dangerous.

5 Read Text 3.4 and then answer **Questions 5a** and **5b**.

Text 3.4

Whether we like it or not, the influence and use of AI is growing rapidly all over the world, it will soon impact most areas of human life. But is AI a friend or a foe? Is it going to steal jobs from humans, making millions of people redundant? Or is it going to lead to much greater efficiency in several fields, including scientific research, healthcare and finance? 5

There is no doubt that AI can process and analyse huge amounts of data faster than any human. For example, there are now AI programs that aid doctors in the faster diagnosis of complex illnesses such as cancer by spotting symptoms that are too subtle to be visible to the human eye. Unlike humans, AI needs no rest or sick days, and it can work 24/7 with no holidays required 10 to prevent burnout. AI is also happy to do the mundane, repetitive jobs that humans hate. In terms of leisure, AI can improve customer experiences through its use of algorithms – for example, predicting programmes that may be of interest or making personalised recommendations when shopping online. 15

With all these positive impacts, why do so many people have reservations about the creeping use of AI in everyday life? One reason is that behind every AI program are real people, so the AI they launch could reinforce and perpetuate human bias, leading to discrimination. AI also lacks human empathy and sensitivity which, in the long term, could result in a less caring 20 and more brutal society. In addition to this, AI is completely reliant on the work of humans for its source material, which raises the question, how will those humans be rewarded or recognised for their work? There are big issues with patents as well as the copyright of music, literature and art.

The biggest concern, however, is the speed with which AI is increasingly 25 influencing our lives. Many argue that AI could be the end of civilisation because our increasing reliance on it will make us more vulnerable to cyber-attacks, leading swiftly to social unrest. By growing too rapidly, there is a real risk that these important issues will not be addressed until it is too late.

a According to Text 3.4, in what ways could AI improve life for humans and what are the perceived threats?

Use continuous writing (not note form) and use your own words as far as possible.

Your summary should not be more than 120 words.

Up to 10 marks are available for reading and up to 5 marks for writing. [15]

b Assess the writer's attitude to the rapid growth of AI.

Use **three** details from Text 3.4 to support your answer. [5]

REFLECTION

What have you found to be the most difficult things about writing a summary? List three challenges of summary writing and explain how you plan to overcome them.

Now think about how easy you find it to assess a writer's attitude. How confident do you feel about responding to these questions, on a scale of 1–5 (where 1 is not confident at all and 5 is very confident)? If you answered 1–4, try to identify what you found difficult and make brief notes of any ideas you have for improving this skill.

SELF-ASSESSMENT CHECKLIST

Let's revisit the learning objectives for this unit.
Decide how confident you are with each statement.

Now I can	Show it	Needs more work	Almost there	Confident to move on
read a text and offer an overview of it	Name the reading strategy you use when you form an overview of a text.			
identify the main ideas in a text	List the main points you included in your response to Text 3.4.			
differentiate between main ideas and supporting details or examples	List the details and examples you left out of your response to Text 3.4.			
reorganise and synthesise ideas	Explain what 'synthesising ideas' means.			
remodel a text in my own words	What are the key things to remember when remodelling the text in a summary?			
produce a coherent piece of new writing in response to a given task.	What are the important things to remember when using connectives in a summary?			

Exam practice 2

The questions in this section will allow you to demonstrate the skills you have covered in Unit 3 and will help you prepare for your assessment.

The following text and questions have example student responses and commentaries. Write your own responses to the questions first, then compare your responses to the examples. Read the commentaries carefully and see whether any of the comments apply to your response, then revise your responses to improve them.

Text A: Overtourism in Venice

Overtourism boils down to the simple fact of too many people visiting the same place at the same time and Venice is, sadly, a prime example. Some 20 million visitors flood in each year; on its busiest days, around 120,000 people visit this city which is home to just 55,000 permanent residents. Many of these tourists stick to the most famous landmarks – the Rialto Bridge, St Mark's Square – further concentrating numbers into a tiny footprint. This damages Venice's fragile buildings, strains its infrastructure, inhibits local people from going about their business and, frankly, makes for a woeful visitor experience, too. Nobody benefits, not even the tourists.   5

The reasons behind overtourism in Venice are complex and manifold. [. . .]   10
The rapid growth of low cost aviation, cruise ships and peer-to-peer home sharing platforms are all guilty parties. The rise of the day tripper is a huge problem too. Ironically, no one seems to dedicate time to seeing this timeless city. Of the 20 million people who come to Venice each year, only half sleep here, which is why hotel stays have dropped two thirds over the past 25 years. Many have   15
poured off a cruise ship – on some days as many as 44,000 cruise passengers come to the city – or are on a whirlwind tour of Italy. Some stay for just a few hours, see little, buy a few trinkets and leave. They bring no economic benefit to the city in this way.

[. . .]

Obviously, life for those remaining local residents is impaired by this influx of day   20
trippers and tourists. On any given day they are forced to negotiate crowds and put up with noisy wheelie suitcases, selfie sticks and often disrespectful behaviour – swimming in canals, picnicking on bridges – as they try to go about their daily lives. They see the city they love being littered [. . .] and reflect on how the artisan spirit of the city has been eroded.   25

Overtourism's impact stretches beyond quality of life though. With time, overtourism changes the balance of economic incentives for a whole range of businesses that are important in defining the character of a city. The food, the goods in the shops, even the music being played in bars all lean towards the tourist taste, and increasingly fail to cater for local people.   30

It also becomes difficult to find work in any field outside of tourism. And what do you find when poor employment opportunities, the rising cost of living, [...] and a reduced quality of life combine? Depopulation. Venice has become too expensive, too impractical and just too much of a tourist theme park for most residents to be able to stay.

35

From responsibletravel.com

Question 1

a   According to Text A, what are the problems caused by overtourism in Venice to the local people and the city itself?

Use continuous writing (not note form) and use your own words as far as possible.

Your summary should not be more than 120 words.

Up to 10 marks are available for reading and up to 5 marks for writing.   [15]

Example student response 1	Examiner comments
Tourists are a real nuisance in Venice and the locals just hate them. It's because they behave like yobs running around the city yelling and making a noise. Venice is really beautiful so it's a shame that the tourists are ruining it with their noisy behaviour. I went to Vencie once and it was so crowded it was rubbish. It's a really expensive place too so most tourists can't afford to buy anything when they get there. In my opinion the writer thinks Venice is a rip-off and tourists should not go there. I know this because the writer says Venice is like a tourist theme park which shows that it is expensive and not a good place to go on holiday.	This response lacks focus on both the text and the task. It makes three relevant points – that the tourists are noisy, that Venice is crowded, and that Venice is expensive – but there is too much irrelevant material included (that is not in the text). Also, the student includes personal comments about their own experience of visiting Venice, and the writer's opinion of Venice, which are not relevant in a summary task.

To improve this response, the student needs to focus solely on the text, extracting the relevant main points and organising them coherently. All personal opinions and comments should be removed and there should be no material included that is not in the text. The tone also needs to be more formal and the writing style more plain.

4/15 marks |

Example student response 2	Examiner comments
Several problems are caused by the excessive number of tourists visiting the small city of Venice. The most obvious issue is overcrowding, especially in the more popular areas such as the Rialto Bridge and St Marks Square. The overcrowding also damages Venice's fragile buildings and strains its infrastructure. Because so many tourists are day trippers, they bring no economic benefit to the city as they just buy a few trinkets and leave. The residents are affected because they are forced to negotiate crowds and put up with disrespectful behaviour such as swimming in canals and littering. As a result the artisan spirit of the city has been eroded. It is also hard for the locals to find any work outside the tourism industry.	This response makes seven relevant content points – crowding, damaging the buildings, putting pressure on infrastructure, no economic contribution, disrespectful behaviour, changing the artisan spirit, shortage of jobs outside tourism. However, the range of points is undermined by the tendency to lift whole phrases directly from the text. This weakens the evidence of reading understanding. For example, does the student understand what 'strains its infrastructure' or 'the artisan spirit of the city' mean? Changing or remodelling the language, for example 'puts pressure on the roads and services' or 'the city's love of skilled artisans' shows the examiner that understanding is secure.
	This response is an appropriate length, but it includes some unnecessary examples, such as the Rialto Bridge and St Mark's Square, and also the examples of disrespectful behaviour. Cutting out the examples would allow more room for further main points. There is also repetition of the 'crowds' point which should have been spotted in the planning stage.
	8/15 marks
Example student response 3	**Examiner comments**
There are a variety of problems caused by overtourism in Venice. Firstly the most popular tourist spots get excessively crowded as there are 120 000 tourists each day compared to only 55 000 permanent residents. These crowds end up damaging the old historic buildings as well as putting pressure on the infrastructure such as roads. The tourists are often poorly behaved, dropping litter and creating large amounts of noise. Most of them are off cruise ships and don't spend any money in the city at all. This means they don't contribute to the economic health of the city. Locals get affected by this because the city they love is unrecognisable. The small craft shops have been replaced by touristy restaurants and outlets changing the atmosphere of the city. It has also made the city very expensive to live in yet most of the jobs available are low paid ones in hospitality to cater to the tourist market. This results in many locals leaving Venice as they no longer enjoy living there.	This is generally a well-focused response which is written in the student's own words. It makes 11 relevant content points – crowding, tourists outnumbering locals, damage to buildings, pressure on infrastructure, poor behaviour/litter, noise, not spending money, change in city's spirit/atmosphere, retail outlets cater to tourists, expensive to live there, only jobs in tourism – which is a wide range.
	The student uses their own words and shows sound reading understanding. It is fluently written and organises the points well, avoiding repetition.
	There is some extra material in this response (the cruise ship detail, for example). It is rather long at 169 words and would benefit from a more concise style in places.
	14/15 marks

b Assess the writer's attitude to the behaviour of tourists in Venice.

Use **three** details from Text A to support your answer. [5]

Example student response 1	Examiner comments
The writer seems very frustrated about how tourists crowd into the most popular areas in Venice and destroy enjoyment of the city for everyone – including themselves. This is evident in the comment 'and, frankly, makes for a woeful visitor experience, too' as the word 'frankly' indicates that he/she is going to say something brutally honest and the word 'woeful' is a strong way of showing how awful and intrusive he/she thinks the overcrowding is. The writer also shows he/she is sympathetic to the locals about the appalling behaviour of the tourists when he/she lists all the disrespectful things that they do such as 'swimming in canals' and 'littering'. This behaviour would spoil the environment for the locals who want to go about their daily lives. Even the 'noisy wheelie suitcases' are referred to which shows the writer feels so angry with the tourists that everything they do is annoying for him or her, as tourists can't really help the noise made by suitcases but the writer responds as though they are doing it deliberately.	This response assesses three attitudes: frustration, sympathy for the locals and anger. Each attitude is fully explored and supported with concise and well-chosen textual details. The answer focuses sharply on the question. 5/5 marks
Example student response 2	**Examiner comments**
The writer shows genuine affection for the city of Venice and wants all the tourists to stay at home because they spoil the city for everyone who lives in it due to their bad behaviour. The writer is worried that all the locals will leave the city and go to live somewhere else because it is too expensive to live there.	This response does identify some of the writer's attitudes but is not focused on the question (the behaviour of tourists). Instead, the candidate focuses on the writer's attitude to Venice and the locals without linking any of the comments to the tourists' behaviour other than a brief assertion that they 'spoil the city'. However, this is not supported by any details from the text. To improve the answer, the student needs to read the question more carefully to ensure the answer is more relevant. 1/5 marks
Example student response 3	**Examiner comments**
The writer is really angry with tourists in Venice because they behave badly. The evidence from the text is 'selfie sticks and often disrespectful behaviour – swimming in canals, picnicking on bridges – as they try to go about their daily lives. They see the city they love being littered'. This shows the writer is angry and wishes the tourists would behave better when they visit Venice as their behaviour is unacceptable. The writer gets really annoyed about the tourists and thinks they spoil the city.	In this response, only one attitude is identified: anger (repeated twice, then framed as annoyance). There is some evidence from the text (a rather long quotation), but the answer does not use the evidence to fully assess the writer's attitude to the behaviour of tourists. To improve the answer, the student should think of different attitudes to explore and illustrate with evidence from the text. 2/5 marks

4 Analysing and explaining writers' effects

In this unit, you will practise analysing and evaluating the ways in which writers use language for deliberate impact on the reader. You will learn how to recognise interesting words and phrases, consider their meanings within the context of the text and then explore how the chosen language helps shape the reader's response to the text by creating atmosphere, conveying attitudes or evoking an emotional response. You will also have opportunities to practise answering exam-style questions that ask about writer's effects and understand how these are assessed.

4.1 Understanding meanings and effects

When approaching a question that asks about writer's effects, it is a good idea to start with the meanings of words – a skill you have already practised in comprehension questions. Once you have worked out the meaning of a word, it is much easier to explain its effect. Try this step-by-step strategy:

- Read the whole sentence or paragraph (whichever is appropriate to the question).

- Make connections with other information in the text.

- Predict possible meanings.

- Replace the unfamiliar word with your own word(s) in the sentence to see if they fit.

1   Read Text 4.1. Work out the meanings of the words in bold (suffocating, the horizon, reckless, parched, aimlessly, barely and remote), using the strategy outlined above.

> **Text 4.1**
>
> As the sun rose in the sky, the air became thicker and more **suffocating**, making Sybille feel as though she couldn't breathe properly. The dusty road stretched ahead endlessly, meeting **the horizon** and making it impossible to predict how far she needed to walk. Heading into the wilderness without checking the fuel in the car had been **reckless** enough, but only taking one small bottle of water was unforgiveable. Her **parched** throat felt as though it was starting to close up. She stumbled forward **aimlessly** with no idea of what she was hoping to achieve, as the road she had taken was **barely** used, so any chance of rescue was **remote**.
>
> 5

It is important to remember that words with similar meanings can often have subtle differences that impact the reader's understanding of a text. When you choose language to analyse in an exam situation, you must offer meanings that move beyond the literal and show nuanced understanding of the language.

≪ RECALL AND CONNECT 1 ≪

What are 'nuances'? Choose three words with similar meanings and explain the nuance of each of them to show how their meanings have subtle differences.

2   Choose the best word from the options in each sentence to show full understanding of the context.

   a   The pages of the ancient book were faded and . . . [parched / dry / dehydrated].

   b   The narrow road . . . [spanned / meandered / turned] up the side of the hill.

   c   Frowning, she silently . . . [observed / watched / viewed] as he disappeared into the crowds.

   d   . . . [Wobbling / Shaking / Jittering] uncertainly, the little boy pedalled his bicycle along the path.

   e   As the dark clouds gathered in the sky above, huge drops of rain [whacked / pelted / thumped] the roofs of the houses below.

Writers choose language carefully for a variety of reasons. They may use a hook to grab the reader's interest; they may use sensory images to build a sense of foreboding or emotive language to evoke feelings of shock or empathy in the reader. Techniques such as foreshadowing and flashbacks also help the reader make connections within the text.

3   Read Text 4.2 – the opening to a narrative text.

> **Text 4.2**
>
> All at once, my right cheek and ear are coated in a fine damp mist, and reflexively I jerk my head away. Rain? In the Namibian desert? In winter? My mind accelerates from neutral to nimble, creating and rejecting explanations at blinding speed. The sky is a typical Namibia azure blue. There is not a wisp of cloud. So it isn't rain then. Has a passing bird pooped on me? No, it's not a bird either. Because in that same split-second I understand exactly why my cheek is suddenly wet. This is not good. I can see the culprit in my peripheral vision.   5
>
> From *Africa Bites: Scrapes and Escapes in the African Bush* by Lloyd T. Camp

UNDERSTAND THESE TERMS

- emotive language
- evoke
- flashback
- foreboding
- foreshadowing
- hook
- sensory image

a   What hook does the writer use to arouse and sustain the reader's interest?

b   How does the writer build a sense of foreboding in this extract?

4   Use **one** example from the text below to explain how the writer uses language to suggest their fear.

Use your own words in your explanation.

'All at once, my right cheek and ear are coated in a fine damp mist, and reflexively I jerk my head away. Rain? In the Namibian desert? In winter? My mind accelerates from neutral to nimble, creating and rejecting explanations at blinding speed.'   [5]

4.2 Language chosen for deliberate impact

Many words have similar meanings, but there are subtle differences that deepen the reader's understanding of the text. Look at this example, in which different verb choices change the reader's perception of a character's mood or attitude:

- The little girl bounced down the stairs.
- The little girl crept down the stairs.
- The little girl tripped down the stairs.
- The little girl slid down the stairs.
- The little girl tottered down the stairs.

1 Change the verb 'ran' in the following sentence to create different meanings.

- Reem **ran** down the road towards the school gates.

For example:

- Reem **raced** down the road towards the school gates.

Try to create five new sentences. Note down how the reader's understanding of Reem's attitude to school subtly shifts in each sentence.

Connotations of words allow you to explore shades of meaning in a text, considering the different associations they may have. This means engaging with a writer's language at word and phrase level. It is helpful to start by thinking about word connotations in terms of whether they are positive, negative or neutral.

2 Look at each group of three words below and organise them into positive, neutral or negative connotations.

  a inquiring / interested / nosy

  b weird / unconventional / unique

  c ambitious / power-hungry / driven

Connotations can also be linked to symbolism. For example, the word 'blue' is often associated with feeling sad, while the word 'fire' may be associated with feelings of anger or passion.

3 What symbolic associations can you think of for the following words?

  a green

  b storm

  c crown

  d shadow

  e white

You should also be able to recognise when a writer has deliberately chosen emotive language to provoke a response in the reader. This may be to encourage them to empathise with a character or influence their response to a situation.

Look at this example of emotive language:

- He was desperate to get the funding he needed to escape to a new country to study.

Now look at the same information written in plainer language:

- His ambition was to be accepted by a university overseas with a full scholarship.

4 Rewrite these sentences in plainer language.

  a Fans were left aghast by the shock result in the cup final.

  b As the storm wreaked havoc over the neighbourhood, several family homes in its path were left in tatters.

UNDERSTAND THESE TERMS

- connotation
- provoke

---

5   Rewrite these sentences using emotive language.

  a   She smiled as she saw the view from her balcony when she arrived on her first holiday in a number of years.

  b   He was worried about how much it would cost to repair his car after the traffic collision.

≪ RECALL AND CONNECT 2 ≪

Why is it important to use your own words in questions that use the command word 'explain'?

---

6   Use **one** example from the text below to explain how the writer uses language to suggest how the building site is affecting local people.

Use your own words in your explanation.

'The town's residents are at breaking point as a relentless stream of lorries travelling to and from the construction site continues to choke the roads, spewing dust into the air. What should be a 15-minute school run has turned into an hour-long battle with cars crawling along bumper-to-bumper, engines idling and tempers flaring. One local described it as "A never-ending nightmare".'   [5]

4.3 Exploring figurative language

Remember that figurative language encompasses several key literary devices, including metaphor, simile, personification, hyperbole, onomatopoeia and alliteration. Writers often use figurative language to create deeper meaning, so being able to explain why a writer decides to use a word figuratively rather than using plainer language means you have started to move from explaining meanings in context to exploring the effects of deliberate language choices.

1   Look at the following pairs of sentences. Explain the effect of the figurative language in the first sentence compared to the plainer language used in the second. For example:

- The sun glared down unrelentingly for the whole day.
- The sun shone down unrelentingly for the whole day.

The word 'glared' in sentence one makes the sun sound hostile and angry – as though it wants to harm people, whereas the word 'shone' in the second sentence is a more positive word, so doesn't convey how unpleasant the heat was.

  a   Food prices for essential goods have rocketed over the last few months.

  Food prices for essential goods have risen over the last few months.

  b   An outdoor classroom offers an enchanting environment in which children can learn.

  An outdoor classroom offers an attractive environment in which children can learn.

UNDERSTAND THESE TERMS

- figurative language
- metaphor
- simile
- personification
- hyperbole
- onomatopoeia
- alliteration

TIP

Remember that identifying literary devices alone is not enough to answer a question. You need to include it in an explanation and analysis. For example: 'This use of personification makes the rain sound as though it is being intentionally hostile and deliberately destructive.'

c   Commuting to the office each day in rush hour was draining his energy.

Commuting to the office in rush hour each day was reducing his energy.

d   As the lift shuddered to a halt in between the 20th and 21st floors, they groaned with frustration.

As the lift came to a halt in between the 20th and 21st floors, they groaned with frustration.

When writers use sensory language, it appeals to the reader's direct experiences of the world: how we see, hear, smell, feel or taste something. Using visual, auditory, olfactory, tactile or gustatory imagery enriches descriptive writing, allowing the writer to shape the reader's response more directly. When considering why a writer has used a particular type of imagery, you should not only explore the meaning of the language in the context of the text but also analyse it to explain the impact it has on the reader, or how it helps the reader's understanding.

2   Read Text 4.3, then complete the tasks.

> **Text 4.3**
>
> The lighthouse stood solemnly on the rocky cliff, its weathered masonry bleached by the salt spraying relentlessly against it from the churning seas below. Howling like a wild animal, the wind battered the small, shuttered windows, but the lighthouse remained standing – a guardian in the storm.

a   Explain why the writer describes the wind as 'howling like a wild animal'.

b   Explain why the writer describes the lighthouse as 'a guardian in the storm'.

3   Read Text 4.4 and answer the questions.

> **Text 4.4**
>
> He waited at the small, rural station on its single concrete platform – a corrugated metal hut offering the only source of defence from the fierce rays of the midday sun. It was like being inside an oven as the suffocating heat continued to rise and clog up his lungs.
>
> In the distance, a small, black speck appeared in the hazy air; he gazed   5
> hopefully at it as it slowly transformed into a long, dark python slithering its way towards the station. The tracks started to hum gently with a high soothing ring. As the train got nearer it increased in pitch as the vibrations intensified into a frightening crescendo and the train roared into the station. A rush of wind hit his face, the acrid stench of diesel filling his mouth and   10
> nostrils as the brakes screeched, bringing the train to a stop.

a   What does the word 'defence' suggest about the way the man views the metal hut on the platform?

b   What is the effect of the image 'a small, black speck appeared' to describe the train?

c   What does the metaphor 'a long, dark python slithering' suggest about the train's movement towards the station?

TIP

When analysing imagery, remember that you do not have to explain every single word. Focus on what the image as a whole suggests, and if you do not understand some of the words, just consider the ones that you do understand in your response.

d Explain how the writer uses auditory imagery to create effect when describing the train getting closer to the station.

e Choose three examples of sensory imagery used in the final sentence to describe the man's physical response to the train arriving. Focus on sound, smell and touch.

One of the writer's effect questions will ask you to choose one language example from a short extract to explain how the writer uses language for deliberate impact. Remember to choose an example of interesting language to ensure that you can write in enough detail for the 5 marks available. Choose a phrase and break it down so you can offer meanings of individual words as well as the phrase as a whole, before going on to consider the effects. The mark scheme requires 'clear understanding' for higher marks, so make sure you choose an example that you fully understand.

4 Read Text 4.5 and answer the questions below.

> **Text 4.5**
>
> The city of Petra, nestled within the rugged canyons and desert landscapes of southwestern Jordan, holds a rich tapestry of history woven by the Nabateans, an Arab Bedouin tribe native to the region. Established as a bustling trading post by these resourceful people, Petra flourished as a vital nexus centre for commerce during the Hellenistic and Roman periods.   5
>
> In its prime, Petra served as a bustling crossroads where caravans converged, laden with precious cargoes from distant lands. Here, the incense of Arabia, the silks of China, and the spices of India changed hands, fuelling the vibrant economy of the region. Situated at the   10 junction of vital trade routes linking Arabia, Egypt, and Syria-Phoenicia, Petra became a hub of cultural exchange and commercial activity, drawing merchants and travellers from far and wide.
>
> The Nabateans, adept at harnessing the wealth flowing through their city, amassed considerable riches and established Petra as a   15 symbol of their prosperity and ingenuity. However, their success also attracted the attention of external powers seeking to exploit their wealth. In 312 B.C., the Greek Empire, envious of Petra's prosperity, launched a fateful attack on the city, marking the first recorded reference to Petra in history.   20
>
> From jordan-travel.com

a Why does the writer use the word 'bustling' (line 7) rather than 'busy' to describe Petra as a trading post in the past?   [2]

b Explain what the writer suggests about the impact of trade with other countries in the phrase:

'fuelling the vibrant economy of the region' (line 10).   [3]

c   Use **one** example from the text below to explain how the writer uses language to suggest the impact of the Nabateans' successful trade.

Use your own words in your explanation.

'The Nabateans, adept at harnessing the wealth flowing through their city, amassed considerable riches and established Petra as a symbol of their prosperity and ingenuity. However, their success also attracted the attention of external powers seeking to exploit their wealth.'   [5]

5   Read Text 4.6 and answer the questions.

Text 4.6

The spaghetti was done.

Hearing the alarm she'd set on her phone, Rika took her eyes from the report draft filling her computer screen. Wading through the warm wheaty-smelling vapour to grasp the handles of the pan, she poured out its contents into the colander inside the sink. The stainless steel of the sink buckled,   5
making a sound like a drum being struck, reverberating at her waist. A great plume of steam rose up, whitening her entire field of vision, before dispersing throughout her late-night kitchen with its single-plate hob. The steam wafted up to her cheeks and nose, wetting her skin. So intensely was the spaghetti glistening that it looked as it if were alive.   10

From *Butter* by Asako Yusuki

---

a   Why does the writer use the word 'wading' (line 3) rather than 'moving' to describe Rika as she lifts the saucepan?   [2]

b   Explain what the writer suggests about the noise the sink makes in the phrase:

'a sound like a drum being struck, reverberating' (line 6).   [3]

c   Use **one** example from the text below to explain how the writer uses language to suggest how serious the writer is about cooking this dish.

Use your own words in your explanation.

'A great plume of steam rose up, whitening her entire field of vision, before dispersing throughout her late-night kitchen with its single-plate hob. The steam wafted up to her cheeks and nose, wetting her skin. So intensely was the spaghetti glistening that it looked as it if were alive.'   [5]

4.4 Explaining how writers achieve effects and influence readers

The extended writer's effects question asks you to look at an extract from a longer text and choose three examples of interesting words or phrases to analyse. This question requires a longer response, to show your understanding of the ways in which the writer uses language to create deliberate effects.

The mark scheme for this question mentions some key aspects of the response, including:

- the ability to select powerful or unusual words
- providing words/phrases that carry connotations additional to general meaning
- the ability to explain images.

This means you must select words and phrases that offer sufficient opportunities for analysis and exploration. Avoid plainer language, as this is unlikely to offer enough scope to match the descriptors in the upper levels of the mark scheme.

Look at this adapted version of the mark scheme for the extended writer's effect question.

TIP

Remember to read the writer's effects questions carefully. If a question asks for one example, carefully select one phrase to discuss. If a question asks for three examples, you must explore three interesting words and phrases.

Level	Marks	Description
5	9–10	Words/phrases are precisely selected, including imagery which is imaginatively explained. The response offers analysis which considers both meanings and word associations to explain clearly why the writer used the language.
4	7–8	Words/phrases are carefully selected, including some imagery, and meanings are securely explained within the context of the text. The response offers some analysis of imagery and word associations.
3	5–6	Appropriate words/phrases are chosen. Some meanings are explained but attempts to explain effects are basic.
2	3–4	Some inappropriate words/phrases are chosen. Explanations are general and slight with a tendency to repeat the language of the text or simply identify literary devices.
1	1–2	Word/phrase choices lack relevance. Comments show limited understanding.

1 Look at the task below and the two sample responses.

> Choose **three** powerful words or phrases from the extract below to analyse how the writer uses language to suggest how the landscape changes as evening approaches.
>
> **Use your own words in your explanation.**
>
> 'As the vast desert landscape turned a glowing shade of deep orangey red, the sun sank slowly beneath the horizon, casting its final light across the sand. Silhouetted against the evening sky a lonely cactus stood in the distance as a cooling breeze began to stir the sand causing waves of ripples to rise and fall lapping at their feet like the edge of a golden sea. The air, once dry and still, carried the faint scent of dust and sun-baked earth, whistling through the low shrubs and desert flowers. Everything felt endless: ancient, like the desert itself.'   [10]

Answer A

The writer uses the phrase 'deep orangey red' to describe the colour of the landscape. This shows the reader how the landscape looks beautiful, and orange and red are bright colours that we would associate with beauty. Orange is also something we associate with fruit and being healthy. The writer also says, 'across the sand', which shows that the desert is very sandy and is probably vast too. We would think of a beach when we hear the word 'sand', so it has happy connotations for the reader and makes them think of holidays and nice weather. This uses the reader's memories to make an effect. The third example is 'lapping at their feet', which makes us think they are still at the beach, as we associate this with water such as the sea. It makes the sand sound like water which is interesting because sand is dry, whereas water is wet.

Answer B

The writer describes the desert during the evening showing that the light is fading and the landscape changes. The use of colour in 'turned a glowing shade of deep orangey red' is effective as it uses powerful colours that we associate with fire and strong feelings. It heightens the sensation of the sun's power showing that even as it sinks, its influence over the landscape is still intense. It creates a natural sense of beauty too. The description 'Silhouetted against the evening sky a lonely cactus stood in the distance' also creates an eerie atmosphere as the landscape is so bare and 'silhouetted' shows that the cactus appears dark against the red sky as a bold and striking shape. The fact that it is 'lonely' adds to the slightly eerie atmosphere and makes the cactus sound introspective. Finally, the phrase 'endless: ancient, like the desert itself' makes the desert sound like a force of nature which has existed long before humans and is therefore much more powerful. It also adds a mysterious tone, suggesting the profound effect of watching sunset in this place.

a   Evaluate each response using the mark scheme descriptors.
    Which is the better response?

b   Rewrite the lower-level answer using the mark scheme descriptors to help you improve it. You can make different language choices or add words to them.

2   Choose **three** powerful words or phrases from the extract below to analyse how the writer uses language to describe cooking.

> 'She sliced off a knob of the Calpis[1] with a knife and perched it on top, then watched as the pale-yellow solid gently began to change colour, spreading out to the sides and turning golden, mingling with the fish eggs. The full, milky aroma of the butter married with the salty marine tang of the roe as the scent of the dish went rising up to her face, and she breathed it deeply into her lungs.'   [10]

GLOSSARY
[1]**Calpis:** a luxury brand of butter

3   Read Text 4.7 and then answer the questions.

> **Text 4.7**
>
> **The rope is jammed.**
>
> It's stuck way above us in a cleft of rock, and without it there is no hope of escaping from this mountain. We look at each other in horror. It has been a very gruelling day … and it just got worse. […]

Among the high jumble of weathered rock, in the gloaming, my friends and I consider our plight. Our last remaining bottle of drinking water is mysteriously yellowed and foul [. . .]. We must have used a filthy bottle. We are exhausted, beaten up by the weather, by disappointment, by hunger and thirst. A ghostly blue moon is starting to cast long eerie mountain shadows over the desert plain below. The plain of sanctuary. We are running out of time. It's all gone wrong.   5

[. . .]

The plan to fly our paragliders off Spitzkoppe, an imposing red granite pinnacle and the highest free-standing peak in Namibia has turned out to be fantastically misconceived. We knew it might be, but the three of us feel bulletproof and have a youthful disregard for consequence. It was worth a try and here we are. [. . .]   10
It's a tougher climb than we expected and it has gone on all day, the merciless sun beating down upon our backs and heads, reflecting into our faces off the crystalline rock. [. . .] Negotiating the claustrophobic cracks and chimneys is sweaty, cramped work, but it pales in comparison to the exposed final few pitches of coarse granite where the world drops away below your feet and where you have to trust the sinuous rope to hold you if you make a false move.   15

From *Africa Bites: Scrapes and Escapes in the African Bush* by Lloyd T. Camp

a   Use **one** example from the text below to explain how the writer uses language to suggest the danger the men are in.

Use your own words in your explanation.

'Among the high jumble of weathered rock, in the gloaming, my friends and I consider our plight. Our last remaining bottle of drinking water is mysteriously yellowed and foul. We must have used a filthy bottle. We are exhausted, beaten up by the weather, by disappointment, by hunger and thirst. A ghostly blue moon is starting to cast long eerie mountain shadows over the desert plain below.'   [5]

b   Choose **three** powerful words or phrases from the extract below to analyse how the writer uses language to describe the difficulty of the climb.

'The plan to fly our paragliders off Spitzkoppe, an imposing red granite pinnacle and the highest free-standing peak in Namibia has turned out to be fantastically misconceived. We knew it might be, but the three of us feel bulletproof and have a youthful disregard for consequence. It was worth a try and here we are. [. . .] It's a tougher climb than we expected and it has gone on all day, the merciless sun beating down upon our backs and heads, reflecting into our faces off the crystalline rock. [. . .] Negotiating the claustrophobic cracks and chimneys is sweaty, cramped work, but it pales in comparison to the exposed final few pitches of coarse granite where the world drops away below your feet. . .   [10]

REFLECTION

How will working out and explaining the meanings of words/phrases in context help you tackle writer's effects questions in the exam? What is the most useful skill you have gained to help you analyse the effects of language? What do you need to work on further to improve your understanding of how to explain writer's effects?

SELF-ASSESSMENT CHECKLIST

Let's revisit the learning objectives for this unit.
Decide how confident you are with each statement.

Now I can	Show it	Needs more work	Almost there	Confident to move on
explain what is meant by a 'writer's effect'	Write a definition of a writer's effect for a younger student just starting the IGCSE course.			
describe the ways in which word choices affect meaning	Explain the difference between these phrases: • Her clothes were worn. • Her clothes were ragged.			
explain how the connotations of words and phrases influence a reader	Give three examples of a word or phrase with a meaning that goes beyond its literal meaning. Explain any word connotations.			
identify figurative language techniques and explain their effect on a reader	Find good examples of each of the literary devices you have learnt. Explain why you think they are effective.			
describe how writers use figurative language to create atmosphere	Explain the effect of these descriptions: • The trees cast eerie shadows in the moonlight. • The moon's light sparkled on the still, dark waters.			
analyse how and why writers use sensory language	Explain the different types of sensory language and find an example for each one in this unit.			
recognise different types of questions that ask about writers' effects	Find an example of each type of questions which assess writers' effects in this unit.			
understand how the mark schemes are applied to particular questions.	What is the difference between explaining and analysing?			

5 Extended response to reading

SKILLS FOCUS

In this unit you will:

- select, evaluate and use relevant ideas and details from a text to create a new piece of writing
- develop ideas from a text using inference
- understand the features of articles, speeches, journals, letters, interviews and reports
- write for different audiences and purposes using appropriate language
- create a convincing voice using a range of vocabulary and sentence structures.

EXAM SKILLS FOCUS

In this unit you will:

- consider connections between concepts
- understand the importance of keeping to time when planning and writing an extended response to reading
- know what a good response looks like
- understand how the mark scheme applies to extended response tasks.

In this unit, you will practise writing extended pieces in response to narrative reading texts, which involves both reading and writing skills. While doing so, you will learn how to make connections between concepts – understanding what is required for a successful response and applying the learning you have gained from across the whole course. You will evaluate some example responses and take a closer look at how marks are allocated for this question in the exam. You will also understand how to plan and write your own response within the time constraints of the exam.

5.1 Conventions of text types

The extended response to reading tasks draws together the reading skills you have developed throughout the previous units. In this question you need to:

- scan the text to find the relevant ideas and details to address each bullet point

- understand explicit information in the text to include appropriate ideas

- understand implicit information in the text to offer evaluation of the ideas and make inferences

- understand the figurative language used in the text so you can express the ideas in your own words and adapt the language to create an appropriate voice.

> ## ≪ RECALL AND CONNECT 1 ≪
>
> Write down definitions of explicit meaning and implicit meaning.

You will be asked to frame your response in one of several possible text types, including article, letter, speech, report, interview and journal. All of these are structured slightly differently and demonstrate a variety of features. It is useful to understand these features and feel confident about applying them to your writing.

1   Which of the following features matches each of these text types?

   article   letter   report   speech   interview   journal

   a   Uses a headline and subheadings and may use quotes from witnesses or interested parties.

   b   Welcomes the audience and addresses them directly. Uses rhetorical features to keep them interested. May have an informal or formal tone, or a mixture of both.

   c   Opens with an appropriate greeting and directly addresses the reader. Includes a suitable sign-off at the end. Can vary in formality.

   d   Written in a personal, reflective tone using paragraphs to structure and develop a sequence of ideas.

   e   May have a title and use subheadings. Uses a formal tone and develops a logical sequence of paragraphs.

   f   May have an introduction to introduce a guest. Written as a series of questions and answers.

2   Identify the text types of the following short extracts and list the features you identified that helped your decision.

   a   **Text 5.1**

   Good morning, everyone. Today I am here to explain what we can all do to make our local communities cleaner, safer and more pleasant for all of us. First of all, I want to ask you a question: how many of you are sick of seeing litter on the pavements and in storm drains?

b   **Text 5.2**

Dear Sir,

I am writing to express my concern about the changes made to the local bus timetables, which mean that there will no longer be a service arriving in the local town by 9 a.m. Many village residents rely on this service to get to work, so this will cause considerable difficulties and could result in some losing their jobs.

c   **Text 5.3**

A new facility for Sunny Town!

A new community centre was opened in Sunny Town yesterday, aiming to hold events designed to bring the community together. Mayor Brownridge, who opened the centre, praised the initiative as 'a fantastic facility that will particularly benefit young people and local families'. The centre will host several events each week and has published a programme on its website.

d   **Text 5.4**

Investigation into residents' complaints

After evaluating the concerns raised by residents, the residential block was inspected and found to be inadequate in terms of fire safety and garbage disposal. Many complaints were received by the local council prior to the commissioning of this study, mostly concerned with fire doors being left open or residents failing to use the communal bins, instead leaving their garbage on landings and walkways.

e   **Text 5.5**

Javid: I'd like to welcome our guest, Alda, this morning. She is here to tell us all about her latest campaign to improve sporting opportunities for girls in this district. Hello Alda, it's great to meet you at last.

Alda: Thanks for inviting me.

Javid: Tell us why you are so interested in improving sporting opportunities for girls?

Alda: My interest in girls' sport began when I was very young and got told that I couldn't play football because it was for boys only. I felt outraged.

f   **Text 5.6**

Looking back, I know I shouldn't have felt so nervous. The interview went as well as I could have expected. They were warm and friendly, and I could give good answers to all their questions, based on my work experience and what I learnt in my college course. No matter what the outcome is, I feel proud of myself. If I don't get the job, I will be sad, but I will trust the process and accept that it wasn't the right role for me.

≪ RECALL AND CONNECT 2 ≪

List as many conventions of formal and informal writing as you can.

5.2 Evaluating and using ideas from a text

UNDERSTAND THIS TERM

- voice

For a successful extended response to reading, you need to evaluate the information in the text in order to select material that is appropriate to the task. So, before you start writing, you need to read both the task and the source text carefully and then plan what you will include in your response. Remember – you can follow a five-step process for this planning stage:

1   Read the source text closely and form an overview of what it is about.

2   Read the task carefully so you understand what ideas you need to select.

3   Decide which ideas from the text are relevant to each bullet point and write a rough plan.

4   Note any small details from the text that could be used to support your ideas.

5   Plan how you are going to adapt the ideas and perspective in the text to suit the purpose, audience and voice of your own writing.

The extended response question is worth 20 of the 80 marks available for Paper 1. It is important that you time the examination carefully so that you leave 30 minutes for this question – a quarter of the exam time. Spend 10 minutes on the planning stage, scanning the text and selecting the ideas to use for each bullet point, then spend 20 minutes writing your response.

Read Text 5.7 – an extract from a longer text about a newly appointed headmaster and his wife.

Text 5.7

Michael Obi's hopes were fulfilled much earlier than he had expected. He was appointed Headmaster of Ndume Central School in January 1949. It had always been an unprogressive school so the authorities decided to send a young and energetic man to run it. Obi accepted this responsibility with enthusiasm. He has many wonderful ideas and this was an opportunity to put them into practice.   5
He had had sound secondary school education which designated him a 'pivotal teacher' in the official records and set him apart from the other headmasters. He was outspoken in his condemnation of those older and often less-educated ones.

'We shall make a good job of it, shan't we, Nancy?' Michael Obi asked his young   10
wife when they heard the joyful news of his promotion.

'We shall do our best,' she replied. 'We shall have such beautiful gardens and everything will be just modern and delightful…' In their two years of married life she had become completely infected by his passion for 'modern methods' and his denigration of 'these old and superannuated people in the teaching field   15 who would be better employed as traders in the Onitsha market'. She began to see herself already as the admired wife of the young headmaster, the queen of the school.

The wives of the other teachers would envy her position. She would set the fashion in everything ... Then suddenly it occurred to her that there might not be other wives. Wavering between hope and fear, she asked her husband, looking anxiously at him.   20

'All our colleagues are young and unmarried,' he said with enthusiasm which for once she did not share. 'Which is a good thing,' he continued.

'Why?'   25

'Why? They will give all their time and energy to the school.'

Nancy was downcast. For a few minutes she became sceptical about the new school; but it was only for a few minutes. Her little personal misfortune could not blind her to her husband's happy prospects. She looked at him as he sat folded up in a chair. He was stoop-shouldered and looked frail. But he sometimes surprised   30 people with sudden bursts of physical energy. In his present posture, however, all his bodily strength seemed to have retired between his deep-set eyes, giving them an extraordinary power of penetration. He was only twenty-six but looked thirty or more.

From 'Dead Men's Path' by Chinua Achebe

1   Imagine you have been asked to write a journal entry as if you were Michael Obi, considering the impact of your new role as headmaster on your wife, Nancy. In your response, you have been asked to include:

- Nancy's reaction to the news that you have been appointed
- what she is looking forward to about being a headmaster's wife
- how you think she will cope with the challenges when they move.

a   Identify the main ideas from Text 5.7 that are relevant to each bullet point.

b   Identify any smaller details from the text that will support your ideas.

At least one bullet point in the task is likely to require you to look for clues in the text to develop through inference. In the example above, it is bullet 3, which asks how Michael thinks Nancy will cope with the challenges of the move to Ndume School. To respond to this bullet point, you might use the following ideas from the text:

- 'The wives of the other teachers would envy her position. She would set the fashion in everything . . . Then suddenly it occurred to her that there might not be other wives'.
- '"All our colleagues are young and unmarried," he said with enthusiasm which for once she did not share.'
- 'Nancy was downcast. For a few minutes she became sceptical about the new school; but it was only for a few minutes.'

Here is an example of how you could modify and adapt these ideas to create a convincing voice for Michal Obi when addressing the third bullet point:

I am worried that Nancy may get lonely when we move to the new school. I noticed her dismay when I revealed that most of the other staff at the school are unmarried men. She looked very disappointed, although she quickly hid it from me as she always puts my needs before her own. I know she is a young woman who enjoys making friends, and I think she assumed that she would be some sort of 'queen bee' among the other young wives at the school. I do feel some sympathy for her as she may find herself rather isolated, but we must be brave and consider our duties first. I will have to make sure that I involve her in the daily work of running the school to keep her busy.

2   Make notes on how you would need to adapt the ideas you have identified in the text, and the perspective from which these ideas are presented, to suit the purpose, audience and voice required by the task.

3   You are Nancy. Write a letter to a close friend telling her about Michael's new job. Use ideas and details from the text to explain:

- how you feel about your husband's new appointment as headmaster

- what you are most looking forward to about being a headmaster's wife

- your concerns about how Michael will cope with his new role.

Use your own words to write Nancy's letter.

Write about 250–300 words.

Up to 10 marks are available for reading and up to 10 marks for writing.   [20]

> **TIP**
>
> There may be more than one character in a text, and you could be asked to write from the perspective of any of the characters. This means selecting appropriate ideas and modifying them by viewing the events through that character's eyes.

5.3 Developing ideas

Once you have identified the ideas from the text that you want to use in a response, you need to think about how you can develop them to extend the response and show your writing skills to their best advantage. One of the main ways in which you can do this is by focusing on the voice of your writing and bringing your own ideas to what the person whose viewpoint you are expressing would think about the situation.

Read Text 5.8 – a non-fiction narrative describing a tourist called Zandile's experience of accompanying a guide on a crocodile hunt in Australia. The events are viewed through Zandile's eyes and include her thoughts and feelings about the experience.

> **Text 5.8**
>
> As we set out on the swamp in our rickety wooden canoe, the sun was dipping low over the horizon. The reeds were thick at first which helped stabilise the canoe, but as we broke through them into the more open water, it started to tilt precariously with the slightest movement. My heart was thumping furiously, and I began to regret my stupid decision to sign up to an expensive night-time expedition to hunt crocodiles deep in the Australian outback. 'Just get through it, Zandile,' I thought to myself. 'It must be perfectly safe, or they would get closed down.'   5

As we paddled into the increasingly dark waters, my guide, Brock, explained
that if we were lucky, we'd come across saltwater crocodiles further up the   10
creek. He'd seen some 'slides' there earlier – the marks left where crocs enter
the water – as well as a pile of wallaby bones, which was all good evidence of
large crocs in the area. 'The mature males can grow up to twenty feet, Zandile,'
Brock announced cheerfully as he swept his torch beam across the murky
waters ahead of us.   15

I'd never seen a crocodile in the wild and was starting to feel very nervous.
The canoe was lurching horribly with each paddle, its wooden planks
groaning as though protesting at our combined weight. There were thin
gaps between some of the boards which allowed water to trickle in and pool
around my trembling feet. I gripped the edge with white knuckles certain that   20
at any moment a pair of cold reptilian eyes would rise from the water.

Trying to distract myself, I asked Brock how he could assess the size of a
crocodile. He ignored me at first then muttered, 'The eyes . . . how far apart
they are . . .' as he continued to wave his torch beam around in the blackness.
I decided to shut up.   25

We continued our rocking journey through the inky water with tangled tree
roots below the surface dangerously ensnaring the canoe intermittently.
Around us the swamp whispered and clicked with the buzzing of insects and
sudden frantic bursts of croaks. Every sound was magnified, echoing off the
water and reverberating around my head. The darkness was like a wet cloth   30
pressing down on me and the humidity was making me feel faint. I was being
eaten alive by mosquitoes and there was no repellent on board.

'I can see one!' Brock whispered excitedly, pointing ahead of the canoe.
I leaned forward as much as I dared as the canoe tilted dangerously but could
see nothing. 'Aw, lost it, mate', said Brock. 'Let's see if it resurfaces. That was a   35
whopper.' I couldn't tell whether he was just trying to frighten me as we hung
around for a bit – me hoping fervently that the crocodile wouldn't reappear.

Finally, we continued paddling, but it wasn't long before Brock tried to wind
me up again. I'd suggested that the whole concept of hunting crocodiles
in the dark was crazy. He initially denied it but then admitted that it was   40
possible that our canoe could be mistaken for a fellow croc, attacked from
the underside and flipped over. He told me if this happened, I should swim
away quickly but avoid moving my arms and legs. He continued scanning the
waters while I digested this completely useless advice. The whole expedition
was absurd. If there were crocs in this stupid swamp, we couldn't see them   45
anyway because it was so dark. We had nothing but a battered up wooden
canoe with one paddle, a torch and a small bottle of water: no first aid box,
rope, life jackets or even a stun gun. I told Brock to turn around immediately
and return me to civilisation.

1 Read the exam-style task below. Make a note of the voice, style, audience and purpose that you should include in your response.

> You are Zandile. After complaining to the Health and Safety department of the tourist board about your trip, you have been asked to submit a report outlining your concerns about the expedition to hunt crocodiles.
>
> You should explain:
>
> - your concerns about the safety of the expedition
>
> - your impressions of Brock's attitude and behaviour as a guide
>
> - how the company could improve the experience for customers in the future.
>
> Use your own words to write Zandile's report.
>
> Up to 10 marks are available for reading and up to 10 marks for writing.

2 Look at part of an example plan a student has made for the first bullet point. Copy the plan and add as many details as you can to develop the last three ideas.

Bullet point	Ideas and details from the text	Development
Concerns about the safety of the expedition	The timing – it's night-time so dark.	Limits the possibility to see crocodiles and makes the trip far more dangerous if anything happens.
	The canoe – made of wood, old and unstable, gaps which let water in, no spare paddle.	An engine is needed if a quick escape becomes necessary. A large croc could flip the canoe over or completely splinter it.
	The environment – the water is murky; there are tree roots snaring the canoe.	
	Health of the passenger – the heat and humidity, mosquitoes, lack of food and water.	
	Lack of safety equipment – no first-aid kit, life jackets or stun gun.	

3 Extend this plan to make notes for the second and third bullet points:

- your impressions of Brock's attitude and behaviour as a guide

- how the company could improve the experience for customers in the future.

Time yourself to ensure that you take no more than ten minutes to complete your plan.

Even when you are asked to write in the same voice as the narrator in the text, you need to adapt and develop the voice to meet the needs of the purpose and audience. For example, in the task you have been working through here, you need to adapt and modify the informal and personal tone used in the text to write a formal report.

Creating and maintaining an appropriate voice is essential to achieving a higher level in the reading mark scheme. To gain top marks (9–10) in reading skills, you need to show a 'consistent and convincing voice'.

4   Read this paragraph from a sample student response addressing bullet point 1. This would score a level 2 (3–4 marks) in the reading mark scheme, where the descriptors are 'The voice might be inappropriate' and 'some brief, straightforward references to the text are made'.

> Zandile hated being in the middle of a swamp with water trickling in and the canoe lurching horribly from side-to-side. She thought Brock was rude and mean. She got eaten by mosquitoes and there was no insect repellent. It wasn't safe for Zandile on that old canoe at all.

Rewrite the paragraph to bring it up to a level 4 ('An appropriate voice is used' and 'a good range of ideas is evident / some ideas are developed') or level 5 ('A consistent and convincing voice is used' and 'A wide range of ideas/developed ideas are sustained and well related to the text').

5   Use your plan to write a full response to the question.

You are Zandile. After complaining to the Health and Safety department of the tourist board about your trip, you have been asked to submit a report outlining your concerns about the expedition to hunt crocodiles.

You should explain:

* your concerns about the safety of the expedition

* your impressions of Brock's attitude and behaviour as a guide

* how the company could improve the experience for customers in the future.

Use your own words to write Zandile's report.

Up to 10 marks are available for reading and up to 10 marks for writing.   [20]

Remember that you could be asked to write in a different voice from the original narrator of a source text. This means changing the perspective – considering events through someone else's eyes and using clues in the text to create a convincing voice for them. This is an important part of evaluating and developing ideas in a text.

UNDERSTAND THIS TERM
• perspective

6   In Text 5.7, the narrator is Zandile, but she mentions another person – Brock. To change the perspective to Brock's, you need to consider why he may assume that a tourist would like to be taken in an old rickety wooden canoe rather than a modern, motorised boat. You may also like to consider whether, as suggested in the text, he is deliberately trying to scare Zandile and think about why he would do that. For example, when he claims to have seen a 'whopper' that Zandile does not see, is he telling the truth or is he joking to entertain her?

Make a plan for the following task. Remember to adapt the material to adopt Brock's perspective.

You are Brock. Following a complaint from Zandile, you are asked to attend an interview with a Health and Safety officer from the Australian Tourist Board about the trips you offer tourists to hunt crocodiles. The interviewer asks three questions only:

- What do you aim to offer tourists when you take them on a night-time crocodile hunt?

- Why do you think your behaviour during the trip may have led to a complaint?

- What improvements can you make to ensure tourists feel safer in future?

7 Look at the two example student responses to the task in Activity 6, and the adapted mark schemes below. Use the mark schemes to decide which is most successful and why.

Reading

Level	Marks	Description
5	9–10	Uses a wide range of ideas with a strong sense of purpose and a convincing voice. All three bullets are well covered with supporting details used throughout.
4	7–8	Uses a good range of ideas with a clear sense of purpose and an appropriate voice. All three bullets are covered with frequent details.
3	5–6	Uses a range of straightforward ideas but little development, so the text is used mechanically with no sense of purpose. The bullets are addressed unevenly, and the voice is plain.
2	3–4	Makes brief and straightforward references to the text with reliance on lifting. Limited focus on the bullets and the voice may be inappropriate.
1	1–2	Little sense of engagement with the text. May be mostly copied.

Writing

Level	Marks	Description
5	9–10	Effective style and structure Good range of vocabulary and language suits audience and purpose.
4	7–8	Mostly fluent and effective style with ideas well sequenced. Some precise use of vocabulary and effective language for audience and purpose.
3	5–6	A plain style and sequence tends to follow original narrative. Adequate vocabulary and clear language.
2	3–4	Inconsistent style and poorly sequenced. Simple vocabulary and awkward expression.
1	1–2	Brief and undeveloped or copied sections from text.

Answer A

Interviewer: What do you aim to offer tourists when you take them on a night-time crocodile hunt?

Brock: My aim is to take them on a night-time expedition to hunt crocodiles deep in the Australian outback. I explain that I have seen slides, which are the marks left by crocodiles when they enter the water and so I know they will be in the creek. I tell them that mature males can grow to 20 feet so they will get excited. I then paddle them down the creek and try to spot them. I shine my torch on the water and look for their eyes, and I tell the tourist when I can see one.

Interviewer: Why do you think your behaviour during the trip may have led to a complaint?

Brock: I think Zandile was afraid of the crocodiles, and I didn't do enough to reassure her that things were okay. The canoe was rocking a lot so she was scared she would fall in, but I did tell her what to do if that happened. It was dark and I don't think she liked the noises in the creek. She moaned about not having a life vest, which I thought was a bit much and she didn't like my canoe because it was leaking.

Interviewer: What improvements do you have planned to make tourists feel safer in future?

Brock: I will buy a bigger boat with an engine and put life vests on the tourists and a first aid kit on the boat. I will also do the trips in the daylight so the tourists can see more crocodiles. I will stop fooling around so much and be more polite to the tourists.

Answer B

Interviewer: Hello Brock. Thank you for attending this interview. We need to find out a bit more about the trips you are offering to tourists to decide whether you are taking health and safety seriously enough.

Brock: Sure mate, ask me anything you want.

Interviewer: What do you aim to offer tourists when you take them on a night-time crocodile hunt?

Brock: My aim is to give people a good time. They all want to be like Crocodile Dundee, don't they, so I put them in an old wooden canoe and take them on a swampy creek right out in the middle of nowhere as it gets dark. I use a paddle and deliberately sway the canoe, so they think they're going to get thrown off. It's all part of the act. There's been no sighting of crocs in that creek for 30 years, but they don't know that. I take them at night to make it even more scary with the insects buzzing and the frogs croaking, and I tell them we are looking for crocs over 20 feet long – that's always a good wind-up and gets their hearts racing! I even pretend to see one but say it went back under when they try to see it too. I only take one torch, so they are left in the dark a bit.

Interviewer: Why do you think your behaviour during the trip may have led to a complaint?

Brock: Well, I guess that Zandile took it all a bit too seriously. I always think they'll know I'm winding them up when I tell them to swim for the shore without moving their arms and legs, but she really believed me. I mean, the canoe leaks as well so it's obvious I wouldn't really use it in a creek with real crocs around. I was so busy shining my torch on the way ahead, I didn't notice that she was showing real signs of fear and holding on to that canoe so tightly. I didn't notice all those mozzie bites she got either – I guess I should have told her to use some repellent before we set off. Her face when I told her that a croc might flip the canoe was a picture! She really fell for that one. I guess she just didn't get my sense of humour. I'm guessing I scared her a bit too much though.

Interviewer: What improvements do you have planned to make tourists feel safer in future?

Brock: I guess I go a bit too far so need to reign it in a bit. In future, I'll put a bit of mozzie spray around the boat and maybe carry a first aid kit. I could patch up the canoe a bit to stop the leaks and stop fooling around to rock it or maybe get a better canoe with an outboard engine in case I drop the paddle. I suppose the tourists should be wearing a life jacket too. I don't want to tell them there's no crocs though, as that would spoil the trip completely but if they feel a bit safer, they'll enjoy the hunt more. The trip is just a fantasy, but the tourists love it. There's no danger really and it makes them feel like a hero.

8 You are Zandile. A few months after your trip, you enter a travel writing competition in which you write an article about a disastrous experience when travelling overseas. You decide to write about your crocodile-hunting trip with Brock. In your article you should explain:

- what happened to make the trip so disastrous

- your impressions of Brock and his skills as a guide

- how Brock could improve the customer experience in future.

Use your own words to write Zandile's article.

Write about 250–300 words.

Up to 10 marks are available for reading and up to 10 marks for writing.   [20]

REFLECTION

How confident did you feel about answering extended response questions? Are there any areas of writing an extended reading response that you still feel unsure about? How did the five-stage process help you to plan an extended reading response? Look at it again and think about any stages where you could strengthen your performance.

SELF-ASSESSMENT CHECKLIST

Let's revisit the skills focus for this unit.

Now I can	Show it	Needs more work	Almost there	Confident to move on
select, evaluate and use relevant ideas and details from a text to create a new piece of writing	Explain how to use the question to plan your response.			
develop ideas from a text using inference	Choose a paragraph from Text 5.8 and rewrite it from Brock's perspective, developing the ideas by using inference.			
select appropriate information from texts for different purposes	Explain what reading strategy you need to use to effectively select appropriate information from texts and why.			
understand the features of articles, speeches, journals, letters, interviews and reports	Write a set of revision cards outlining the key features of each text type.			
write for different audiences and purposes using appropriate language	Make a list of all the different audiences and purposes you have written for in this unit.			
create a convincing voice using a range of vocabulary and sentence structures	Give an example of where you have used textual information to create a convincing voice while doing this unit.			

CONTINUED

Now I can	Show it	Needs more work	Almost there	Confident to move on
understand connections between concepts	Find three examples of where you have connected the concept of selecting appropriate ideas with the concept of inference in your answers to the questions in this unit.			
understand the importance of keeping to time while incorporating time to plan my response	Summarise how much time you should spend on planning and writing the extended response task in the exam.			
understand how mark schemes are used to assess the extended response to reading.	Explain how a level 3 reading response which uses the text 'mechanically' could be improved.			

Exam practice 3

The questions in this section will allow you to demonstrate the skills you have covered in Units 4 and 5 and will help you prepare for your assessment.

The following text and questions have example student responses and commentaries. Write your own responses to the questions first, then compare your responses to the examples. Read the commentaries carefully and see whether any of the comments apply to your response, then revise your responses to improve them.

Read Text A then answer **Questions 1(a)–(b)** and **2**.

Text A

Gap year adventures

Rene Bliszko happily waved to her parents as she approached the airport security desks on a warm September day. She had no reservations about the long flight ahead of her and only looked forward to escaping her mother's constant interference in her life. She had finished her A Level examinations and was finally free to do some travelling and explore the world before returning in six months   5 to prepare for her college course. Rene smiled happily to herself as she joined the long, slow-moving queue.

By Christmas she was having second thoughts: her bank account had become dangerously low, and she'd had to email her parents to ask for some funds. They had agreed but asked some tricky questions about where all her savings had gone,   10 as well as the generous donation they had given her before she left. She was deliberately vague in her replies, not wanting to tell them about all her adventures on remote islands, diving off boats and partying through the night. She hadn't kept to her daily budget at all but had decided to find much cheaper hostels to stay in for the remainder of her trip.   15

That's how she arrived at the Monkey Puzzle Hostel – a basic place, but one that was close to the centre of the chaotic and rambling city she was currently visiting. The area was a bit run-down, but it was the best she could afford on her meagre budget. She had managed to reserve a bunk in a girls' dormitory and planned to stay for a couple of weeks.   20

The dormitory was grim and claustrophobic, packed tight with rusty metal bunk beds arranged in suffocatingly narrow rows. The mattresses sagged like tired sponges, and the threadbare sheets clung to them like discarded rags, riddled with holes. Several light bulbs were missing or flickering erratically, casting jittery shadows across the walls. The bins, long since abandoned by the so-called cleaning   25 rota – overflowed with plastic bottles and crumpled wrappers, spilling their contents across the cracked, grimy floor tiles. The windows were grimy with metal bars making them impossible to open.

After dumping her backpack on her bed, Rene wandered down to the common room – a communal area where residents could gather and socialise. The walls were covered in flyers advertising excursions and tours to places of interest, and even car shares down to the coast on weekends. Then she spied a small cork board which had some adverts for local jobs. Rene wasn't sure whether her visa allowed her to do any paid work but when she asked Kai, the guy at the hostel reception desk, he said it would be fine to apply anyway. 30 / 35

The best thing about the hostel was the cheap internet access, so she spent the afternoon catching up with her travel blog and catching up with her friends in their group chats.

By the weekend, Rene felt completely at home. Money was still tight, but she had found a job working at a local café for a few hours a couple of times a week. She'd even carved out a space for her groceries in the communal fridge wedged between mouldy tomatoes and yoghurts long past their sell-by dates, releasing a sour tang every time the door was opened. Drawn by the sound of loud music, she went into the common room where a lively crowd of newcomers were spilling in. Soon the place was heaving with young people dancing and laughing – even Kai had ditched his reception desk to join the fun. 40 / 45

A few hours later, Rene's heart dropped into her stomach as the common room door swung open and in stormed her parents. Her mother's face was like an army general inspecting the new troops as she barked, 'Who is in charge here? Why has reception been abandoned?' Mrs Bliszko's gaze swept the room like a searchlight until it landed on Rene, half hidden behind a beanbag. With a shriek, she charged across the floor. 'What on earth are you doing in this hovel? You told us you were staying in a decent hotel?' Then she spun to face the rest of the room and declared, 'All of you should be asleep! It's the middle of the night!' 50

Poor Rene was ordered to pack her things and join her parents in their luxury hotel. But not before Mrs Bliszko had inspected every inch of the hostel and declared it a health hazard that should be shut down immediately. 55

Question 1

a   Use **one** example from the text below to explain how the writer uses language to suggest the state of the dormitory.

Use your own words in your explanation.

> 'The dormitory was grim and claustrophobic, packed tight with rusty metal bunk beds arranged in suffocatingly narrow rows. The mattresses sagged like tired sponges, and the threadbare sheets clung to them like discarded rags, riddled with holes. Several light bulbs were missing or flickering erratically casting jittery shadows across the walls.'   [5]

Example student response 1	Examiner comments
The writer uses the phrase 'sagged like tired sponges' to describe the mattresses on the bunk beds. This means that they were too soft and dipped down in the middle. This simile suggests that the mattresses were very worn out from so many people sleeping on them. 'Sagged' gives the impression that they have no resistance at all so would be very uncomfortable to sleep on and not do their job properly and offer a good night's sleep. The use of 'tired sponges' also implies that they may be a bit grubby, as a sponge that has been used for too long has connotations of being unhygienic and harbouring germs. This creates a sense of disgust in the reader that the beds are dirty and unfit for their purpose.	This response offers a clear and precise language example to explain how the writer describes the dormitory. The response offers accurate meanings of the whole phrase as well as considering the connotations of individual words such as 'sagged' and 'sponges', offering some thoughtful analysis of the overall effect on the reader. This is a well-developed answer that can be credited for several clear explanations of meanings and effects, so would be awarded full marks. 5/5 marks
Example student response 2	**Examiner comments**
When the writer describes the sheets as 'discarded rags' it makes it sound like they have been thrown away in the rubbish bin because they are rags not sheets. This makes it sound wasteful because they aren't being used anymore which makes the dormitory sound as though people are being wasteful. But 'rags' also makes the sheets sound as though they are damaged and wouldn't be very nice sheets to have on a bed because they are worn out. It also says the shadows are 'jittery' so they are trembling on the walls which means the shadows are acting as though they are afraid and frightened in the dormitory. This shows an effect on the reader of making the reader feel scared too.	This response offers two examples of how the writer uses language, but only one can be credited. The first example, exploring the phrase 'discarded rags' is the better answer, so is the one that would be credited. The student correctly explains 'discarded' as 'thrown away', but it repeats the word 'rags' instead of explaining it using their own words at this point. The explanation that 'people are being wasteful' is not an accurate or relevant explanation, but the response does go on to explain that the word 'rags' means the sheets are 'damaged' and 'worn out' which is an accurate meaning. The attempt to explain 'jittery' is less successful as it shows some misreading of the text, linking jittering to fear rather than to the annoyance of the flickering light bulbs. Therefore, the explanations of the first chosen example are more successful, so are the ones credited. 2/5 marks

b   Choose **three** powerful words or phrases from the extract below to analyse how the writer uses language to describe Mrs Bliszko's reaction to the hostel.

> 'Her mother's face was like an army general inspecting the new troops as she barked, "Who is in charge here? Why has reception been abandoned?" Mrs Bliszko's gaze swept the room like a searchlight until it landed on Rene, half hidden behind a beanbag. With a shriek, she charged across the floor. "What on earth are you doing in this hovel? You told us you were staying in a decent hotel?" Then she spun to face the rest of the room and declared, "All of you should be asleep! It's the middle of the night!"

Write about 200–250 words.

Up to 10 marks are available for the content of your answer.   [10]

Example student response 1	Examiner comments
The writer says Mrs Bliszko 'barked'. This is a word we would usually associate with guard dogs and it means she made a loud sudden sound so her voice is not very pleasant. It also makes her sound quite fierce and scary. My next example is 'hovel' which is the word she uses to describe the hostel. It makes the hostel sound nasty and as though it is like a hole in the ground or a cave or somewhere where humans shouldn't be living because it's more like a place suitable for animals. It makes the hostel seem disgusting. The next example is 'she spun to face the rest of the room'. The word 'spun' means she turned around really fast. The word 'faced' means she was looking at everybody. It makes it sound as though she is being quite harsh and strict almost like a teacher at the front of the class.	In this response, the student chooses three appropriate words and phrases but does not tackle any imagery, and limits two of the language choices to single words. There is some success in the explanation of the word 'barked', which shows understanding of the meaning as a sudden and unpleasant sound, making Mrs Bliszko sound fierce. The explanation of 'hovel' is less successful – there is some understanding in the hostel sounding 'nasty', but the student misunderstands the explanation of a hovel being a hole or cave or a home for animals. The response improves in the explanation of the phrase 'spun around to face . . .', where meanings are explained accurately and there is an attempt to move on to an effect in the idea of Mrs Bliszko appearing to be strict 'like a teacher'.
	To improve this, the student needs to be more precise in the selection of language examples and include some imagery. The explanations need to be more analytical and think more deeply about word connotations and associations.
	5/10 marks
Example student response 2	**Examiner comments**
Mrs Bliszko is described using language often associated with war, because she goes into battle with the hostel residents. Firstly, she is 'like an army general inspecting the new troops', which implies that she sees herself as someone with a lot of authority and power, and views the young people in the common room as naïve subordinates that she can order around at will. This suggests a huge power imbalance and emphasises how formidable Mrs Bliszko is and how difficult it will be to stand up to her. We are then told that her 'gaze swept the room like a searchlight', which again links to the idea of war and finding the enemy who is hiding as she looks around the room to find her daughter. It shows that she misses nothing and makes her sound almost as though she has superpowers or is like a machine rather than a human being. Her next move is to 'with a shriek, she charged across the floor' which suggests she is like an army battalion moving in on the enemy. 'Charging' has connotations of going into battle and again is associated with military power and links neatly to her being an 'army general'. 'Shriek' is less controlled so suggests that she is slightly more emotional than a military person should be but could also been seen as a battle war cry as she moves in for the fight. These language examples all paint Mrs Bliszko as a strong and determined woman who is intent on rescuing her daughter.	This response offers three clear examples of language choices, all of which are precisely selected. The choices include imagery that the student explains fully, linking the words to meanings and associations such as the military language used throughout the extract. This is used to offer detailed and imaginative analysis of the way Mrs Bliszko is presented in the text and shows clear understanding of why the writer chose the language being analysed. This is a well-developed response which is placed in the highest mark level. 10/10 marks

Question 2

You are Mrs Bliszko. After you have removed Rene from the hostel, you write a letter to the Public Health Officer in the city to demand that the Monkey Puzzle is shut down. In your letter, you should explain:

- your concerns about the poor state of the hostel

- the way the hostel is managed

- what dangers could happen if the hostel remains open.

Use your own words to write Mrs Bliszko's letter.

Write about 250–300 words.

Up to 10 marks are available for reading and up to 10 marks for writing.   [20]

Example student response 1	Examiner comments
Dear Public Health Officer, I am writing to let you know about a hostel for backpackers that operates in your city and which I think should be closed down. I found my daughter in this hostel recently and took her away straight away when I saw how awful it was. The hostel is in a very poor state, with horrible dormitories where the beds are too crammed in together and have saggy mattresses and horrible sheets. The food in the fridge is going off and smells. There are light bulbs missing and some that flicker too. The way the hostel is managed is very bad. When I arrived there was no one on reception and I found the only staff member there just socialising with the young residents instead of looking after them. The place is also dirty and no one gets any cleaning done and the bins are overflowing with plastic bottles and crumpled wrappers spilling their contents on the floor. The music is played too loudly late at night so no one can get any sleep at all. If the hostel remains open, there could be a lot of risks such as rats getting in because of the bins not being emptied. If reception is left unattended strangers could come in and steal things too. Young people still need to be looked after by a responsible adult. I hope that you take my points seriously and close the hostel down soon. Your sincerely Mrs Bliszko	This response shows that the student has read the text reasonably well, but the use of the text is a bit mechanical, as the ideas have not been modified or adapted very much to suit the purpose and audience. The focus on the bullet points is a bit uneven – the third bullet point, which requires some inference and development of ideas, is too brief. The writing is clear but rather plain with some rather long sentences and a tendency to repeat vocabulary. To improve the response, the candidate needs to modify the facts and ideas from the text to create a more convincing voice for Mrs Bliszko. The ideas should be used to show her disgust and determination to get the hostel closed. In the text, she is presented as very domineering and loud, so this should be harnessed in the response to create an appropriate tone for her. In this response, she comes across as quite reasonable and mild. The overall style is too plain, although the expression is clear. Reading: 5/10 marks Writing: 6/10 marks

Example student response 2	Examiner comments
Dear Sir/Madam, I must alert the public health unit to the existence of a dreadful hostel for backpackers, situated in a scruffy area close to the city centre. This hostel is unfit for purpose and puts the health and safety of anyone staying there in grave danger. Firstly, the dormitories are overcrowded and unhygienic, with too many bunk beds and dirty sheets that pose a health risk to the occupants. Not only that, but the windows are barred up and filthy. The lights are bare bulbs with some missing and others that flicker annoyingly. How on earth are people supposed to sleep? As for the mess, I can't even begin to express how disgusting it is – rubbish everywhere you look. And as for the way that the hostel is run – is there even a manager? I met some feeble young man who had deserted his post on reception to party noisily with the children. That common room has messy disorganised noticeboards advertising dodgy trips in old cars – are any safety checks carried out? I was also told that this person, Kai, encouraged my daughter to get a job when she only has a tourist visa. Doesn't he know the law? The place is filthy, with no cleaning rota enforced and mouldy food in the fridge. The whole place stinks. Those young people are just left to run wild when in fact, they need discipline and rules. If this hostel remains open, I fear that something terrible could happen and the blame would lie firmly with you. The electricity is clearly dodgy, which could cause a fire and if that happened the overcrowding and inaccessible windows would mean there is little chance of escape. I'm amazed there hasn't been an outbreak of food poisoning yet and wouldn't be surprised if the place was infested with rats. The lack of security where anyone can walk in is also a dreadful worry for parents like me, as well as those suspect trips and jobs being advertised there. I am relying on you to sort this out and close this place immediately. Yours truly, Mrs Bliszko	This response reveals a thorough reading of the text and uses a wide range of ideas across all three bullet points. The ideas are neatly developed to adapt the perspective to Mrs Bliszko's and create a convincing voice for her. The language used is appropriate in supporting the purpose and audience while capturing her personality. The third bullet point has successfully used the clues in the text to suggest where there are possible dangers for the future occupants in the hostel, showing thorough evaluation of the ideas in the text and the ability to modify them to suit the purpose and audience. The writing is fluent and convincing with precise vocabulary. To improve further, the candidate could offer a little more development when addressing the first bullet point, particularly when complaining about the overcrowding and poor beds. Reading: 9/10 marks Writing: 10/10 marks

Writing

7 Writing skills

In this unit, you will look at the different question types in the Writing paper, which are split into two sections – directed writing and composition. You will also explore mark schemes for the Writing paper and develop an awareness of the criteria against which the different questions are evaluated. You will be provided with a series of simplified mark schemes to help you understand what is required to answer many of the questions in the unit, and to develop this skill of evaluating your own work as you monitor your progress.

7.1 Content and style

Effective writing is dependent on what you write (content) and how you write it (style). In some tasks there will be flexibility in these aspects of your writing, but Question 1(b) in the Writing paper will give you specific guidance. This task requires you to write a 250–350-word response that offers your view of the ideas contained in the source texts. The guidance in the question not only informs the content of your response but also signals the intended audience and purpose of your writing.

Remember that 'audience' means the imagined people/person you are writing for (or to) – for example, students or a newspaper editor. 'Purpose' refers to the reason you are writing – for example, to persuade or inform. Together, the stated audience and purpose in a task give you a clue to the type of language you should use and the structure of your writing. For example:

> Write a letter to persuade your headteacher to allow you to organise a fundraising event.

In this task, you are given a format (a letter), so you know you will need to follow the conventions of a letter. You are also given a purpose (to persuade), so you know you need to include ideas that will encourage the reader to adopt your suggestion, and to use some persuasive language as you do so. You are also given a specific single audience (your headteacher), which suggests you that you should use formal, polite language.

1   Look at the following directed writing task.

> Write a speech to persuade students of the benefits of visiting museums.
>
> Use your own words to write your speech based on what you have read in both Text A and Text B.
>
> In your article you should:
>
> •   outline attitudes to visiting museums
>
> •   explain some of the ways modern museums attract visitors.

   a   Identify the following:

      •   the format you should write in – that is, the type of text you are expected to produce

      •   the audience you are writing for

      •   the purpose specified in this task.

   b   Explain how these things will influence the language you use.

Remember that 'voice' means the personality of your narrator/yourself. You can think of voice in terms of an attitude. For example, you might adopt a serious voice, an optimistic voice or a playful voice. The voice you choose will depend on the purpose and audience of the task.

UNDERSTAND THIS TERM

* voice

2   Look again at the directed writing task Activity 1. Explain what type of voice you might use in a response to this task, and why.

Mark scheme awareness is an important skill to master. It is not just about knowing how the marks are allocated in a question, but also relates to what content should be included, and what skills and techniques should be demonstrated to gain the allocated marks.

In a response to the Writing paper, there is not a single 'right' mark, but a range of 'fair and reasonable' marks that could be awarded. This can make it challenging to accurately assess your own work, but it is still a good idea to understand the general principles of how the mark scheme works.

Question 1(b) is worth 35 marks. It tests reading skills (10 marks) and writing skills (25 marks). Look at this simplified mark scheme for the writing element of this question, which identifies the key features of each level. The phrases in bold are the key descriptions.

Level	Marks	Description
6	22–25	**Highly effective** style, structure, vocabulary
		Almost always accurate spelling punctuation and grammar
5	18–21	**Effective style**, structure, vocabulary
		Mostly accurate spelling punctuation and grammar
4	14–17	**Sometimes effective** style, structure, vocabulary
		Generally accurate spelling punctuation and grammar
3	10–13	**Inconsistent** style, structure, vocabulary
		Frequent errors in spelling punctuation and grammar
2	6–9	**Limited** style, structure, vocabulary
		Persistent errors in spelling punctuation and grammar
1	1–5	**Unclear** expression
		Persistent errors in spelling punctuation and grammar
0	0	**Nothing** to reward

3   Read the following partial responses to the task in Activity 1. Using the marking grid above, suggest which level each response would fall into. Explain why you have awarded this mark.

Answer A

Modern museums are particularly keen to attract a range of visitors, consciously encouraging people from all ages and walks of life to pass through their doors. In recent times, museums have made their exhibits more interactive and eye-catching, with the intention of persuading younger visitors that, far from being dull places to visit, museums are hands-on, inspiring places.

Answer B

museums do lots of ways to attract people sometimes by making the things in the museum look intresting and they also want diffrent people to visit so they are putting out lots of adverts and making things sound exiting, which means that children will come in.

Although it appears on the Writing paper, Question 1(a) assesses reading rather than writing skills, so it is important to make the connection with the skills you have acquired through your reading comprehension. The two assessment objectives you need to focus on are:

- R3 Analyse, evaluate and develop facts, ideas and opinions, using appropriate support from the text

- R4 Demonstrate understanding of how writers achieve effects and influence readers.

≪ RECALL AND CONNECT 1 ≪

Write a brief definition of the command word 'evaluate'.

4   Read this extract from a source text.

> 'Writing letters rather than sending emails or messaging is becoming popular again with some young people. "It's time-consuming, but it's a far more personal way of communicating," explains Cal James. "Taking the time to compose a letter, even a short one, shows that you value the person you're writing to. There's something really exciting about writing a letter – far better than sending a text. It means you have to go to the effort of finding a pen, paper, envelope and stamp, and then posting it. It takes far longer to receive a letter than it does a text, but that's part of its charm."'

Use your own words to evaluate Cal's views on writing letters. Give details from the text to justify your answer.   [5]

5   Use this simplified mark grid to award yourself a level for your response to Activity 4. Remember to look closely at the key descriptions in the statements.

Level	Marks	Description
3	4–5	Clear understanding of the view
		Relevant support (quotations/references)
2	2–3	Some understanding of the view
		Some support (quotations/references)
1	1	Limited understanding of the view

7.2 Text structures

Planning is essential for all the tasks in the Writing paper, especially the longer responses. As part of your planning for Question 1(b) and the composition task you choose, you will need to consider the typical features and structure of the text type you have been asked to write in.

1 **a** Make a plan for a response to the following task. Remember to avoid the small details and instead think about the main events you would include.

> Write a story that begins with the words, 'It was the hardest thing I'd ever done.'

 b Review your plan. How effectively have you sequenced your ideas?

2 Write about 350–450 words on the following question.

Up to 16 marks are available for the content and structure of your answer and up to 24 marks for the style and accuracy of your writing.

Describe being in a hot climate. [40]

3 Look at the mark scheme below, which guides assessment for the content and structure of a composition task – a piece of narrative or descriptive writing. This part of the mark scheme allows for a maximum of 16 marks. Award yourself a level for your response to Activity 2.

Level	Marks	Description
6	14–16	Engaging content; secure structure
5	11–13	Mostly engaging content; well-managed structure
4	8–10	Some development of content; competent structure
3	5–7	Straightforward content; mostly organised structure
2	3–4	Simple content; partially organised structure
1	1–2	Occasionally clear content; ineffective structure
0	0	Nothing to mark

> **TIP**
>
> Time spent planning is always time well spent. Start by thinking about the overall shape of your response, rather than the more detailed aspects such as language.

For the composition task, you will have a choice of four questions – two narrative writing tasks and two descriptive writing tasks. The choices that you make can often help or hinder your response. Some students decide that they will always do one of the descriptive options. Some students decide they will always do one of the narrative options. This approach is not necessarily a good idea, as you may end up choosing a question that is less suited to your skills. Spend a couple of minutes considering all options in the composition section. Be guided by the option that you feel you could bring to life – the one that affords the best opportunity to show off your skills.

> **TIP**
>
> In a pressured exam situation, it is easy to misread instructions, especially when you have options to choose from as with the composition questions. Remember that by the end of the exam, you should only have answered **two** questions: one from Section A, and one from Section B.

4   Look at the following four options from Section B of the Writing paper. Spend two minutes thinking about your skills and preferences then decide which one you would answer and explain why.

1   Describe being in a strange room.

2   Describe visiting a deserted village.

3   Write a story that begins with the words, 'I shouldn't have been here.'

4   Write a story with the title, 'The toughest day'.

REFLECTION

What was your thought process as you completed Activity 4?
How did you eliminate some options?

7.3 Word and sentence choices

An effective written response not only uses accurate spelling and grammar but also shows variety in word choices and sentence structures to create different effects. Remember that 'effects' can mean emotional effects such as tension or excitement, but also effects such as creating a sense of sophistication or clarity.

1   Write a paragraph describing the room you are currently sitting in. Select words that convey the appearance and atmosphere of the room.

Varying sentence types will create interest in your writing and can be used to specific effect. For example, very short sentences can create a sense of tension. Sometimes, the overall effect of mixing different sentence types in a paragraph is to create a rhythm and flow that maintains the reader's interest. Using a blend of the three main sentence types, along with other types such as minor sentences and fragments, prevents your work from sounding repetitive.

≪ RECALL AND CONNECT 2 ≪

Name the three main sentence types. Write an example of each.

---

2   Redraft your response to the previous activity. Experiment with using different sentence types.

When you have finished each piece of writing in the exam, it is important to read it through again to check for inaccuracies and places where it could be improved. In exam conditions, you will only have a small amount of time for this – around five minutes – so you will not be able to make any large structural edits. However, it is advisable to do two things:

- a clarity check, to make sure that your phrasing is clear and makes sense

- a technical check, to ensure the accuracy of your spelling, punctuation and grammar.

TIP

It is useful to have a range of synonyms at your disposal. Spend time in your exam preparation period making sure that you are familiar with a range of synonyms for common words.

UNDERSTAND THIS TERM

- minor sentence

3   Look back at your response to Activity 2 in Topic 7.2. Perform a clarity and a technical check. Amend where necessary.

It is possible to make some content amends in the final stages of an exam, but this is likely to be limited to changing a word or two for greater effect. In an ideal world, you will choose appropriate words as you go along, which means that you are less likely to need to replace them as you edit in the final minutes of the exam.

The good news is that as you revise and practise writing in exam conditions, you become more adept at choosing the right phrases first time around. The same is true of sentence construction.

4   Look again at your response to Activity 2 in Topic 7.2.

•   Replace any less effective words with better synonyms.

•   Check the variety of your sentences and amend them where necessary.

5   Use the following mark scheme to decide which level for style and accuracy your response to Activity 2 in Topic 7.2 fits. Award yourself a mark out of 24.

Level	Marks	Description
6	21–24	Precise vocabulary; varied sentences; highly effective language; almost always accurate grammar
5	17–20	Mostly precise vocabulary; range of sentences; sometimes effective language; generally accurate grammar– some errors
4	13–16	Some precise vocabulary; range of sentences; sometimes effective language; generally accurate grammar – some errors
3	9–12	Simple vocabulary; straightforward sentences; frequent errors of grammar
2	5–8	Frequently imprecise vocabulary and simple sentences; persistent errors of grammar
1	1–4	Limited/imprecise vocabulary and simple sentences; persistent errors of grammar
0	0	Nothing to mark

REFLECTION

Think about the times when you have made errors in the written tasks in this unit. Are most of them the same type of mistake, such as misusing punctuation or repeating words? What might help you to minimise these errors?

SELF-ASSESSMENT CHECKLIST

Let's revisit the learning objectives for this unit.
Decide how confident you are with each statement.

Now I can	Show it	Needs more work	Almost there	Confident to move on
write short texts for specific audiences and purposes	Summarise the approach you took in your response to Activity 2 in Topic 7.2.			
understand and use different language choices for effect	Explain the effects of the language choices you made in your response to Activity 1 in Topic 7.3.			
understand and use different sentence types for effect	Give three examples of varied sentence choices form your response to Activity 1 in Topic 7.3.			
structure texts in different ways	Write a plan for the following task, showing the order of events you would include in a full response: Write a story where an expensive item is broken.			
practise accurate use of spelling, punctuation and grammar.	From your response to Activity 2 in Section 7.2, identify three examples each of accurate spelling, punctuation and grammar.			

8 Directed writing

In this unit, you will practise the skills required to write effective directed writing responses. You will study the two distinct tasks that feature in this section of the exam paper and write in the different formats required. You will practise using details from the source text, following a viewpoint and sequencing responses effectively, as well as using different sentence types to create variety in your writing. This unit offers opportunities to practise all of these skills by completing exam-style questions in timed conditions.

8.1 Evaluating views

In the directed writing section of Paper 2 (Section A), you will be asked to read two texts and then respond to two tasks based on them. The first – Question 1(a) – is a 5-mark question in which you need to evaluate a particular aspect of a short extract from one of the texts. To do this, you will use details from the source to show your understanding. Remember that although this is part of the Writing paper, this task connects with some of the concepts you have covered already in the reading comprehension. You will be tested on your skills of analysis, evaluation and understanding of writer's effects.

≪ RECALL AND CONNECT 1 ≪

Write down three things you can recall about responding to Question 1(a) in the directed writing section of Paper 2.

> **TIP**
>
> Remember – to evaluate means to judge or calculate the quality, importance, amount of value of something.

To evaluate someone's view of a topic, you will need to track their opinion, attitude or ideas across the source text and note how it develops.

1   Text 8.1 is an extract from a longer source that explores attitudes towards learning.

> 'I spent the first year of my IGCSE studies doing some work, but nowhere near enough,' explains Rani. 'But I was playing a lot of sport, too, and sometimes I wouldn't spend enough time on homework. People tell me I'm naturally clever, so I'd assumed that I would do well, but I got quite a shock when I got my mock exam marks. They were much lower than I expected. It was not pleasant when I discovered that all my friends had scored higher than me. I decided to change the way I organised my time. I'm playing less sport now, and hopefully next summer I'll be successful in my final exams.'

   a   Read the text and summarise how Rani's attitude to learning changes.

   b   Identify and list the precise words and phrases that convey Rani's attitudes to learning. Some of these attitudes will be explicit and some implicit.

≪ RECALL AND CONNECT 2 ≪

Write down definitions of 'explicit meaning' and 'implicit meaning'.

> **TIP**
>
> Remember that if a question specifies that you should 'use your own words', you must not simply copy sections of the source text but rather paraphrase or summarise the key information that you are being asked for.

2   Look at the following task related to Text 8.1. Make some notes on what Rani's words suggest about her attitude to learning.

> Use your own words to evaluate Rani's attitude to learning.
> Give details from the text to justify your answer.

3 Look at the following two model responses to the task in Activity 2. Explain why the second response is better than the first one.

Answer A

Rani's attitude to learning is that she did 'nowhere near enough work'. She was playing 'a lot of sport'. This shows she was not working hard enough. Rani also 'assumed that I would do well' which means that she thought she was good enough to pass her mock exams but wasn't. Rani decides to change her attitude to learning when this happened and is now 'organised'. She realises she wasn't taking things seriously enough.

Answer B

Rani's attitude to learning changes over time. Initially, she underestimates how much work she needed to do to be successful, but is able to identify reasons for this, primarily that she was 'playing a lot of sport'. This suggests that Rani is astute enough to pinpoint the causes of her underachievement and clearly values her education enough to alter her lifestyle. She is also honest about how her initial attitudes when she admits that being 'naturally clever' had caused her to arrogantly assume that her ability would mean that she didn't need to work very hard. There is also a sense that Rani is competitive and judges her attainment against her peers, suggesting that pride is partly responsible for the change in her attitude. Rani says she 'decided' to change her attitude which suggests she has a mature and decisive manner when it comes to learning.

The sources you are given in the exam will focus on the same topic. However, they may present different or contrasting arguments, to get you thinking about the subject from different angles. The writer's perspective will be informed by the context from which they are writing.

4 Write a brief account of the context of the writer in the extract from Activity 1. How might this influence the content of their writing?

5 Read this extract from a source text.

> 'When I retired from work, I decided that I wanted to return to university,' Farhan explains. 'I spent a lot of my working life pleasing other people, so I made my mind up to spend the later period of my life back in education doing something for myself. I wanted to learn something new. I think any knowledge is beautiful, but what I really wanted to do was fine art. It was the best thing I did. I met new friends, all of them younger than me, and they have helped me become better at my craft. I've done things I never thought I'd do, and while I'm not the best artist, I'm the happiest.'

Use your own words to evaluate Farhan's feelings about art. Give details from the text to justify your answer. [5]

The sources you are given in the exam are ultimately designed to encourage you to form your own view on a topic.

6 Which of the attitudes conveyed in the extracts from Activities 1 and 5 are closest to your own views about the purpose and value of learning? Explain why.

UNDERSTAND THESE TERMS

- argument
- perspective

TIP

When considering how a writer's context is reflected in their writing, think about their age, gender, life experiences, attitudes and cultural background.

8.2 Responding to a task

In Question 1(b) you are asked to produce a 250–350-word piece of discursive writing that gives your view on a topic. The source texts will present views on that topic, which you can both react to and echo in your response.

UNDERSTAND
THIS TERM

• discursive writing

> **TIP**
>
> Always read both sources carefully before you attempt either of the questions in Section A of the Writing paper. On your first read-through, take time to understand the points and ideas before you decide how to respond to the questions.

This question assesses both reading and writing skills. The reading assessment objectives carry up to 10 marks and connect to the concepts you explored in the reading comprehension units, assessing how well you have understood and used material from the source texts. The writing objectives carry up to 25 marks and assess the way you have shaped and written your response. The question itself will remind you of these mark allocations.

It is important to read the question very carefully, because it will give you clear instructions on how and what you should write.

1   Look at the following example of Question 1(b). Note down:

   a   the format specified

   b   the question focus

   c   the reminder to use ideas from the source texts

   d   specific things to include.

> Write an article offering advice to young people about making the most of their education.
>
> Use your own words to write your article based on what you have read in both Text 8.1 and Text 8.2.
>
> In your article you should:
>
> • outline the different attitudes to education people may have
>
> • explain some of the challenges young people might face during their school years and how best to deal with them.
>
> Write about 250–350 words.
>
> Up to 10 marks are available for reading and up to 25 marks for writing.

2   Now read the full Texts 8.1 and 8.2. Make notes on what they each tell you about:

   • attitudes towards education

   • the challenges of learning.

Text 8.1

Growing up offers many challenges. One of them is education, specifically exams. By the time students are in their teenage years, exams have become central to their education. School becomes more about serious study and preparing for tests. This is a natural and unavoidable aspect of life, and whether you secretly enjoy exams or find them stressful, they're here to stay. It's how you cope with them that is the important bit, as Rani, a 16-year-old student explains. 5

'I spent the first year of my IGCSE studies doing some work, but nowhere near enough,' explains Rani. 'But I was playing a lot of sport, too, and sometimes I wouldn't spend enough time on homework. People tell me I'm naturally clever, so I'd assumed that I would do well, but I got quite a shock when I got my mock exam marks. They were much lower than I expected. It was not pleasant when I discovered that all my friends had scored higher than me. I decided to change the way I organised my time. I'm playing less sport now, and hopefully next summer I'll be successful in my final exams.' 10

There is plenty of advice available on how to prepare for exams and how to cope with the challenges they face, and that is all part of the experience. As well as learning facts and revising, something much bigger is being learned: how to prioritise. Like Rani, many students find that, for the first time in their lives, they have to make sacrifices. They have to commit themselves to study and, for a short time at least, cut back on some of their outside interests in order to succeed. 15 20

Text 8.2

Many people think of education in a narrow sense. When they hear the word 'education', they automatically think of their own experience of school. They picture science lessons, running around a field, and the pressure of exams. For many people, school days were the happiest days of all. For some of us, they were a tough time that we were happy to leave behind. But education is much wider than exams. Education is a lifelong process that is about pursuing something you love. Farhan, an older student, has returned to education after leaving work, and he has found the joy of learning. 5

'I never enjoyed exams. They also used to worry me, and it seemed a very unfair way to discover people's talents,' says Farhan. 'When I retired from work, I decided that I wanted to return to university,' Farhan explains. 'I spent a lot of my working life pleasing other people, so I made my mind up to spend the later period of my life back in education doing something for myself. I wanted to learn something new. I think any knowledge is beautiful, but what I really wanted to do was fine art. It was the best thing I did. I met new friends, all of them younger than me, and they have helped me become better at my craft. I've done things I never thought I'd do, and while I'm not the best artist, I'm the happiest.' 10 15

Farhan's experience tells a deep truth about education: the journey of learning is just as important as exams. Many students see education as a means to an end – a way to get a good job. They measure themselves in terms of grades instead of finding joy in what they are learning. 'It's only now I can see the point of education,' says Farhan. 'It's more about growing your mind and horizons, rather than being the best.' 20

Even in exam conditions, you should allow a couple of minutes to plan your response. This involves making brief notes on the texts and planning the order in which you will present your ideas.

3   Using the task and source texts from Activities 1 and 2, and your notes, decide what your own view is on this topic. What advice would you give to young people about making the most of their education? Write a plan showing:

   • your overall argument – the 'angle' you will take

   • the specific points you will make

   • which parts of the source texts you will echo.

4   Write an article offering advice to young people about making the most of their education.

Use your own words to write your article based on what you have read in both Text 8.1 and Text 8.2.

In your article you should:

   • outline the different attitudes to education people may have

   • explain some of the challenges young people might face during their school years and how best to deal with them.

Write about 250–350 words.

Up to 10 marks are available for the reading and up to 25 marks for writing.   [35]

5   Look at the opening of a successful model response to Activity 4. Read it and make notes to identify:

   • where the writer's view comes through convincingly

   • where material from the sources has been echoed.

> Education is a gift. It is an experience that not every young person around the world is lucky enough to benefit from. Yet, there are times when the experiences of exams can feel a little overwhelming – as if we are studying for studying's sake. most of us have had moments where we question the value of learning; times where we have had to minimise our lives outside of school in order to study. This is understandable. But ultimately, it's the wrong way to look at things. Lost the thrill of learning for its own sake? Read on.

As well as the content of your writing, the style and accuracy of your response is an important part of your response. You should ensure that your ideas, vocabulary and sentence types are all working hard to get the message across in the clearest and most effective way.

6   Look at the model response in Activity 5 and note down:

   • the types of sentences used

   • any word choices you feel are particularly effective and why.

7   Rewrite your response to Activity 4, aiming to improve the content and style of your response.

TIP

Remember to use the bullet points in the question to guide your planning. Double-check that your plan addresses the prompts you are given.

TIP

Do not copy words directly from the sources. Remember, you are creating a new text of your own, based partly on ideas in the sources.

8 Write an article persuading readers that education is about more than just passing exams.

Use your own words to write your article based on what you have read in both Text 8.1 and Text 8.2

In your article you should:

- outline the different attitudes to exams that people have

- explain some of the ways education is viewed by different people.

Write about 250–350 words.

Up to 10 marks are available for reading and up to 25 marks for writing.   [35]

8.3 Presenting your views

In this topic, you will practise offering your own view of an issue in response to an exam task. Part of this is deciding what voice you will use in your writing. You will also practise sequencing your argument – deciding on the most effective order. Once you have planned these broader elements of a response, the smaller aspects of language and rhetorical techniques will also require your attention as you write.

1   Read Texts 8.3 and 8.4 and make notes on what they suggest about:

- attitudes towards our throwaway culture

- the challenges of repairing things.

> **TIP**
>
> Key words such as 'argue' and 'persuade' are used to direct you to the mode of writing you should employ. Remember that argumentative writing is generally supported by facts, evidence and logic. Persuasive writing is similar, but it usually relies more on emotional appeals.

Text 8.3

The world is afflicted by a terrible tendency to throw things away. My local recycling centre is full of things that people simply couldn't be bothered to repair. Last week when I was there, I saw two hairdryers, a laptop, a set of office chairs, a fridge and bags of clothes.

Don't get me wrong – recycling these items is far better than throwing them away, and there are times when we need to dispose of things that can't be salvaged. But it seems to me that our throwaway culture has reached a peak. We are no longer prepared to repair broken appliances or sew up a hole in a jumper. Instead, we bin it – recycle it, if we can – and buy a replacement.   5

'I know why this happens,' explains Jana, an environmental protection officer. 'It's because it takes effort to repair things, and although it's a difficult thing to hear, humans have become less inclined to make an effort. We live in a world where some of us can afford to replace items. In years gone by, people would try to repair things first. Now we just get our money out. The problem with that is that it always creates waste. Not everything can be recycled, and when it can, it still costs energy. It's far more environmentally friendly to repair things.'   10   15

If Jana is right, then what the world needs is a change in approach to repairing items. But maybe it's more than simply an attitude change that's required. Perhaps we have lost the ability to repair things – to mend things in the way our grandparents used to. It's a skill we need to relearn.   20

Text 8.4

Mo Jenkins is a secondary school teacher in Birmingham, England, but at
weekends, he runs a Repair School for his local community. His aim is to
encourage people to repair small items rather than throwing them away. What
started as a small project is now thriving. Every weekend, lots of people from
around the city turn up at the Repair School – housed in a former warehouse –   5
where Mo and his colleagues teach people how to mend things.

'I've always been keen to reduce the number of things we throw away,' explains
Mo. 'I'm a keen environmentalist and it saddens me to see how humans' actions
are harming the planet. I don't blame anybody though – for most people, life is
fast-paced and even people with the best of intentions look for quick solutions.   10
That's why I decided to do something about it and teach people how to perform
small repairs.'

Mo's weekend Repair School was busy when I visited. In one weekend, his repair
team diverted 50 kg of waste, saving it from landfill. Together, the team is trying
to combat throwaway culture and save waste. 'The lifespan of most clothes is   15
three years, mainly because people aren't inclined to repair their clothes. One of
the things we do here is to teach people how to maintain their clothes. I think
making a small effort is essential in the fight against waste,' says Mo.

2   Re-read this extract from Text 8.4:

> 'I've always been keen to reduce the number of things we throw away,' explains
> Mo. 'I'm a keen environmentalist and it saddens me to see how humans' actions
> are harming the planet. I don't blame anybody though – for most people, life is
> fast-paced and even people with the best of intentions look for quick solutions.
> That's why I decided to do something about it and teach people how to perform
> small repairs.'

Use your own words to evaluate Mo's views on repairing items.
Give details from the text to justify your answer.   [5]

REFLECTION

This activity is the third example in this unit of the type of task you will find in
Question 1(a) in the Writing paper. Do you feel your ability to answer this style
of question has improved? Why, or why not? What could you do to further
refine your skills?

Before you start writing a response, you need to decide on your viewpoint.
Remember that the texts you are given are there to help you form a view, and as you
read them, you should think about your own ideas on the issues they cover. It can help
to jot down ideas in the margins of the texts, or underline ideas that you might develop
as your own.

3   Look again at Texts 8.3 and 8.4. Note down your thoughts about the value of
repairing items. Remember that you can use and adapt some of the ideas in the
texts as your own.

4 Write an article to persuade people to repair items rather than throw them away.

Use your own words to write your article based on what you have read in both Text 8.3 and Text 8.4.

In your article you should:

- outline attitudes to items that require repair
- explain some of the challenges people might face when wanting to repair damaged items.

Write about 250–350 words.

Up to 10 marks are available for reading and up to 25 marks for writing.   [35]

When planning a response to a directed writing question, you need to think about its structure – the order in which you will present your points. Remember that if you are spending one hour on Section A of the paper (directed writing), you should spend five to ten minutes planning your response to Question 1(b). In that time, you need to note down your ideas and then work out the best order for them.

The most successful argumentative and persuasive responses build to a climax. This is usually an emotional moment that makes the argument most strongly, especially in persuasive writing. It is best to adopt a committed voice – one that sounds like you feel passionately about the issue.

5 Read this climactic section from a model response to Activity 4. Identify:

- where the strength of the voice comes through
- the use of rhetorical techniques.

making the effort to repair damaged items is not just a gentle pastime. It's a vital part of the war against waste. It's time-consuming and it's not easy, but it's essential.

6 **a** Re-read your own response to Activity 4. Consider the effectiveness of:

- the sequencing of your argument
- the voice you have chosen
- any rhetorical techniques used.

b Rewrite your response, aiming to improve aspects of sequence, voice and anything else you feel requires improvement.

8.4 Writing letters and reports

In part 1(b) of the directed Writing paper, you will be asked to write your response in one of four formats: article, letter, report or speech. You will also be given a clue as to your audience. Both the format and audience will influence the style and language choices in your response.

≪ RECALL AND CONNECT 3 ≪

Consider what you have already learnt about writing for different audiences. How would writing a letter to persuade a relative about the importance of keeping healthy influence the language you would use in a response?

TIP

Remember that some conventional features of articles can help give shape to your response. Consider using a suitable title that captures the overall attitude of your response. Subheadings can also be useful.

TIP

In persuasive writing, rhetorical techniques can create a sense of commitment in your writing, when used appropriately.

UNDERSTAND THESE TERMS

- climax
- rhetorical techniques

1   Write a list of features that you would use in a formal letter.

In persuasive writing, you should use rhetorical techniques to make your argument more effective and convince your reader of your point of view.

2   Write a list of the types of persuasive rhetoric you might use to influence a reader.

3   Spend five minutes reading Texts 8.5 and 8.6. As you read, make notes on the opinions they contain about the length and value of long school holidays.

Text 8.5

This text is an extract from an article by a head teacher.

One of the main issues with school holidays is that they are too long. It's with fond nostalgia that many of us remember the long summer breaks of our youth; we recall them as a golden time of playing out with friends all summer long, the days filled with excitement and adventure. But that's a nice myth we tell ourselves. Our brain conveniently forgets the problems that a long school holiday brings.   5

As a parent myself, I know that long summer holidays are counterproductive. My boys become bored after a fortnight, and while our family life is (I hope) solid and loving, frustration easily sets in, putting those relationships under strain. For some students, this boredom leads to antisocial behaviour. Unsupervised children can become involved in youth crime and activities that endanger themselves and others around them. Long holidays are expensive for parents, too. The free and stimulating activities that happen in school   10
are replaced by costly sports camps and trips into town.

There's also an educational issue with long holidays. Many educationalists confirm that summer learning loss occurs – students forget some of the things they have been taught, and upon returning to school, valuable learning time is lost to re-learning skills that were taught before the break. This is especially true for students from lower-income families. It is clear that shorter and more frequent holidays benefit everyone: parents,   15
teachers and, most of all, students.

Text 8.6

In many European countries, school students enjoy long summer breaks. The length varies from country to country. In France, for example, students enjoy eight weeks away from school. For some students and their parents, this feels like a long time to spend away from education, but for others, it's a perfect time to have experiences that make us into rounded human beings.

Jamal, a student, explained his views on school holidays. 'I love the freedom they bring,' he said. 'I think they're a   5
much-needed break from the pressures of education – a way to refresh yourself and spend time doing things away from the classroom.' Like many students, Jamal uses his holidays to enjoy activities he can't do in school time. 'I enjoy hanging out with my friends. In school, we don't get much time to spend time together, and most evenings are soaked up by study and homework, so the holidays are essential. Life would be very dull if we didn't have the time to socialise.'   10

Saima, a mother of four boys, has mixed views but concedes the importance of a break from school. 'There are times when my boys are bored in a long holiday, but in some ways, that's not a bad thing. Children are quite creative when it comes to it, and they can find ways to entertain themselves. That's an important life skill. I love to see my boys play together and the school holidays is a precious time to do that. Children need that time and freedom to grow as people.'   15

4   Re-read this extract from Text 8.6.

> Saima, a mother of four boys, has mixed views but concedes the importance of a break from school. 'There are times when my boys are bored in a long holiday, but in some ways, that's not a bad thing. Children are quite creative when it comes to it, and they can find ways to entertain themselves. That's an important life skill. I love to see my boys play together and the school holidays is a precious time to do that. Children need that time and freedom to grow as people.'

Use your own words to evaluate Saima's views on school holidays.
Give details from the text to justify your answer.   [5]

5   Write a letter to your headteacher to give your views about the length of school holidays.

Use your own words to write your letter based on what you have read in both Text 8.5 and Text 8.6.

In your letter you should:

• outline attitudes to long school holidays

• explain some of the challenges students face during long school holidays.

Write about 250–350 words.

Up to 10 marks are available for reading and up to 25 marks for writing.   [35]

REFLECTION

How well did you manage your time in the previous three activities?
What, if anything, did you find challenging in completing the tasks in the time given? How might you overcome these problems?

Remember that you can use colons to arrange sentences and create a more formal tone. One way to show variety in your work is to use a range of punctuation.

6   Look at the following model response to Activity 5.

> Students benefit tremendously from long holidays: they recharge their batteries, learn new skills, and deepen their friendships.

Note down what effect has been created by using colons.

7   Look back through your response to Activity 5, checking the accuracy and use of colons. Where appropriate, amend or add colons.

Another text type you may be asked to produce is a report. This, too, is composed of sequenced paragraphs, but there are certain aspects that differentiate a report from other formats.

8   Write down the typical structure, tone and features of a report.

TIP

Do not overuse complex punctuation. A response that uses too many colons and semicolons will not improve your work. In fact, it weakens it. Use colons sparingly and only where it adds to your work.

9   Write a report to persuade your local education authority to either shorten school holidays or keep them as they are.

Use your own words to write your report based on what you have read in both Texts 8.5 and 8.6.

In your report you should:

- outline attitudes to long school holidays

- explain some of the challenges students face during long school holidays.

Write about 250–350 words.

Up to 10 marks are available for reading and up to 25 marks for writing.   [35]

8.5 Writing a speech

A speech is primarily designed to be read aloud. However, in an exam context you should not try to include a lot of spoken language features, as if you were delivering a speech to a live audience.

1   Summarise the conventional ways you might open and close a speech.

As part of your planning, you will need to decide on the voice you will adopt in your response. You will probably feel most comfortable using a voice and opinions that are close to your own. However, you should use your revision and preparation time to perfect your use of voice and perhaps find two or three other voices that you feel you could write well in, if they fit the task better – for example, the voice of an expert adult or that of an upbeat, enthusiastic young person.

2   Look back at Texts 8.5 and 8.6. Write the opening section of a response to the task below. Remember to choose a suitable voice for the purpose and your audience.

> Write a speech to persuade students that they would benefit from shorter and more frequent school holidays.

3   Read Text 8.7 and Text 8.8 and then answer the question.

Write a speech to persuade students of the benefits of visiting museums.

Use your own words to write your speech based on what you have read in both Text 8.7 and Text 8.8.

In your article you should:

- outline attitudes to visiting museums

- explain some of the ways modern museums attract visitors.

Write about 250–350 words.

Up to 10 marks are available for the reading and up to 25 marks for writing.   [35]

Text 8.7

Of all the things I might choose to do when I visit a city, going to a museum is towards the bottom of the list. Why? At the risk of sounding like a philistine, they're boring. There are so many other attractions in a city – beautiful buildings, parks, entertainment, theatres, sports arenas. Museums are quiet, dull and uninspiring places. They are places of the past, and quite often the past is best left where it is. 5

I think my dislike of museums started when I was quite young. My parents would take me to museums and art galleries a couple of times each month. They did it with the best of intentions. They wanted to enrich my knowledge – to give me a cultured upbringing. I loved them for that, but when you're young, there's little fun in a dusty sculpture or a 2,000-year-old pot. They don't do very much. There's excitement in football and gymnastics, but not in an Egyptian bangle. 10

Don't get me wrong – as an adult, I love cultural items. I enjoy finding out about history and civilisations, but I don't enjoy the way museums present these things. Museums put interesting things inside glass cases. They lock them away so you can't really look at them. The museum attendants are lovely people, but they often know very little about the exhibits, so you rely on the small cards of information which are written in dull prose. 15

There's got to be better ways to celebrate culture than locking it up in quiet rooms then forcing you to exit through a gift shop selling the usual rubbish that no one wants. 20

Text 8.8

Visit any modern museum these days and you'll find a group of excited schoolchildren running their hands over interactive exhibits, looking at giant screens or being entertained by a museum employee dressed up as a pharaoh. The dry and vaguely oppressive museums of the past are gone. These days, modern museums positively invite people to touch the objects. 5

Last year, I visited the Science Museum in London. I had to queue to get in. Once inside, my eye was taken by the glitzy appeal of the exhibits. Life-sized space rockets and airplanes sat within touching distance. Interactive screens invited me to explore my fingerprint patterns. A dazzling array of video games from across the decades were waiting for me to play them. It was one of the most enjoyable mornings in recent memory. 10

Museums want people to enjoy their visit, and recent reports suggest that visitors experience positive emotions when they come to a museum. They feel a sense of identity and community. They feel optimistic and hopeful. Museums are inclusive places, and often they're free. They positively encourage people of all ages and backgrounds to visit and can become places of positivity for socially isolated and vulnerable people. 15

4 Look back at the sample mark scheme after Activity 2 in Topic 7.1. What level would you award your response to Activity 3 and why? How might you improve it?

REFLECTION

Which, if any, of the formats for writing (article, letter, report, speech) do you feel most confident with. Why do you think that is? Which ones would you benefit from practising more?

SELF-ASSESSMENT CHECKLIST

Let's revisit the learning objectives for this unit.
Decide how confident you are with each statement.

Now I can	Show it	Needs more work	Almost there	Confident to move on
discuss and evaluate opinions	Look back at one of the Question 1(a) tasks in this unit – write a brief explanation of how you chose and evaluated the information in the given paragraph.			
write articles, reports, letters and speeches, giving opinions	Look back at one of the Question 1(b) tasks in this unit – write down three examples from your response that demonstrate where you have expressed an opinion.			
write for different audiences	Choose two responses to 1(b) tasks you have completed in this unit that are written for different audiences. Using examples from each response, explain how you have used language to suit the audiences.			
use persuasive language	Look back at your Question 1(b) responses in this unit and give five examples of persuasive language you have used.			
use colons for effect.	Look back at your response to Activity 7 in topic 8.4. Choose a sentence where you have used a colon and explain the effect you were trying to create.			

Exam practice 4

The practice questions in this section will allow you to demonstrate the skills you have covered in this unit and will help you prepare for the assessment.

The following questions have example student responses and commentaries. For each task, write your own response first, then compare your answer to the example student response and commentary. Read the commentaries carefully and see whether any of the comments apply to your response also. Use the examiner commentaries to consider how you could improve your response.

Read Texts A and B and then answer **Question 1(a)** and **1(b)**.

Text A: Ageism

Most people fear the ageing process: they want to remain youthful for ever. The number of anti-ageing creams and products on supermarket shelves testify to this very understandable and human desire. Getting older is a natural process and one that cannot be avoided. What makes it harder is not the way we look, but the way society treats and views its older members. Ageism is one of the problems that 5 many older people face, especially in the workplace. Some societies have positive attitudes to their older members: in some cultures, older people are valued for their wisdom and experience.

Age discrimination is a problem all over the world. It's often felt most keenly by older employees and those trying to secure jobs. Theresa, an older person, 10 explained: 'I was advised by a career expert to miss my birth date off my CV and to tone down anything that might suggest my age. I would have thought that workplaces would have valued wisdom and experience. Finding a job has not been easy. Often, I find that I lose out to younger people at interviews – often for a job that I'm more than qualified for.' 15

Theresa's experience is not uncommon. Older workers frequently report being turned down for promotion by their bosses or given less interesting activities to complete than their younger counterparts. Ageism is certainly an issue in many cultures, but there are many companies that value employing people from all ages and walks of life. Research indicates that workforces that have a diverse age range 20 tend to be more resourceful and connect with customers more effectively. It is to be hoped that attitudes are gradually changing.

Text B: Fear of the young

Every generation seems to assume that the current generation is worse than the previous one – more degenerate, less intelligent, more unreliable. Each successive group of people has probably always assumed that younger people are a disappointment – a generation that is somehow letting the side down. This view is not an unusual one and it's not limited to the current day. 5
In fact, Greek philosopher, Aristotle, complained in the 4th century BCE that young people 'think they know everything, and are always quite sure about it'! Modern complaints about young people revolve around excessive phone use and lack of persistence.

Such views are generalised and deeply unhelpful. Of course, there are 10
some young people who will conform to such stereotypes, just as there are some older people who are intolerant, slow-witted and technologically illiterate, but there persists a much broader fear of young people. There is an overriding suspicion that they are addicted to phones, unable to communicate and essentially lazy. Yet time and again, these fears prove 15
unfounded; as each generation matures, they show themselves to be just as effective (or ineffective!) as the last. Nothing really changes in humanity's basic attributes.

However, there is a real price to pay for these prejudices about the youth of today – a lack of trust in the workplace that disadvantages young people. 20
I'm sure, like me, you've heard older workers refer to younger colleagues as 'inexperienced', even when they have spent a couple of years at their job. In many workplaces, there's a general suspicion of younger workers. But perhaps the most appalling thing of all is the way younger workers are paid less than their older counterparts for doing the same job – and often more effectively! 25
Society seems to have an in-built assumption that young people are willing to be talked down to by their older colleagues or given tasks to complete that show a lack of trust on their employer's part.

Question 1

a   Re-read this extract from **Text A:**

> Age discrimination is a problem right across the world. Theresa, an older person, explained: 'I was advised by a career expert to miss my birth date off my CV and to tone down anything that might suggest my age. I would have thought that workplaces would have valued wisdom and experience. Finding a job has not been easy. Often, I find that I lose out to younger people at interviews – often for a job that I'm more than qualified for.'

Use your own words to evaluate Theresa's views on age discrimination. Give details from the text to justify your answer. [5]

b   Write a speech to inform local employers of the challenges faced by younger and older people in the workplace.

Use your own words to write your speech based on what you have read in both Text A and Text B.

In your speech you should:

- outline some of the challenges older and younger people face in the workplace
- explain the benefits of employing older and younger people.

Write about 250–350 words.

Up to 10 marks are available for reading and up to 25 marks for writing.　　　[35]

Example student response	Examiner comments
1a Theresa is disappointed that she was asked to miss her birth date off her CV. She says 'she thought that workplaces would have valued wisdom and experience'. This shows that she thinks she's being discriminated against. Theresa also says that she has missed out on jobs that have gone to youngsters. You can see this when she says 'I lose out to younger people'.	The student has identified relevant parts of the text that show Theresa's thoughts on age discrimination and has used quotations to show this. Their evaluation of these comments is simple – there is no sense that they have understood Theresa's emotional response to discrimination, her mistrust of employers' judgements, her slightly simplistic reasoning about why she may have not been appointed. To improve this response, the student could have addressed these ideas. 2/5 marks
1b Hello Employers. Thank you for listening to my speech, I think that it is best to employ people from all age ranges and I am going to tell you why: it is because as Text A says 'workforces that have a diverse age range tend to be more resourceful.' This proves that it's best to employ old and young people. Another things is that people are happier when they work alongside different types of people. Its boring when you just work with one type of person, you get better conversation and you can ask old people for help if they know more. You can ask young people to do physicle things if they are fitter and stronger. That shows that a mix of people is a good thing. Everybody wins. It means that employers have a happy workforce to. Older people can face challenges. They want to look younger – 'anti-ageing creams and products on supermarket shelves testify to this.' Also, like Theresa says, people dont value wisdom. This is a problem because many old people know lots of things and if you ignore them, then you miss out. Also, old people might not be as fit as young people and might struggle with heavy things. They also might not understand computers and technology, so theyll find that hard but that's why you should have young people there so they can help the old ones understand. Thanks you employers for listning to my speech. I hope you decide to employ people of all ages because its only fair. No one likes being discriminated against and like I say, people can learn a lot from each other.	There are some positive aspects to this response. The student has focused on the question, and spelling and punctuation are mainly accurate. It does meet the word count, too. There are issues, however. The student quotes directly from the texts rather than echoing and reshaping the ideas. The points they make themselves are superficial rather than thoughtful and well argued – their argument is flat. There are occasional misspellings ('listning' and 'physicle') and there are missing apostrophes in places. Some sentences aren't demarcated properly – commas rather than full stops are used – and there is a misused colon in the first paragraph. To improve this response, the student could provide a stronger argument with more ambitious vocabulary. 17/35 marks Reading: 5/10 marks Writing: 12/25 marks

Read Texts C and D and then answer **Question 2(a)** and **2(b)**

Text C: The wild life

Schools are usually happy and highly effective places. But they can also be places of high stress, especially when exam success is given so much emphasis. I enjoyed school, but as a father, I can see how narrow school is. It provides an education to my two girls, often a very good one, but it focuses on a small set of skills, some of which will be of little use to them once they leave school. I can remember asking my own science teachers how much of the syllabus I would really use once I'd left school. He quite rightly told me that academic knowledge was 5 a great thing, and the process of learning difficult concepts was useful training for later life, even if the specific knowledge was never used.

As I say, I enjoyed school, but there were times when the pressure got a bit much. That's when nature saved me. There's a lot to be said for escaping into nature – into the wildlife. Spending time in the wilderness is calming. It takes you away from the demands of life and invites you to slow down and take in the world around you. 10 Once you are free of the madness of modern life, you relax and take pleasure in simplicity. In short, you gain perspective – you come to realise that some of the things we get obsessed about are trivial.

That's why I was delighted to hear about the new types of school that are being set up – wilderness schools. Places where classroom-based learning is replaced by an outdoors experience that uses the natural world to teach children to socialise, understand the world and be happy. That's not to say children at wilderness schools don't 15 learn traditional subjects – they do, but not as intensely and in a way that allows them to explore and learn by discovery and talking, rather than traditional teaching methods. The outdoor world has much to teach our young people, and in a time when our attitude to the environment is deeply worrying, they may be the most valuable lessons our children learn.

Text D: Outdoor learning

The new trend for outdoor learning – so-called wilderness schools – troubles me deeply. Ask 100 parents whether they think their kids should spend more time outdoors and they'll agree, but when it comes down to it, most of those parents would be horrified to watch their children grow up without a thorough knowledge of traditional school subjects and qualifications to go with them.

Wilderness schools claim that they equip their students with a whole host of social skills that they wouldn't 5 necessarily learn in traditional schools, but I'm not sure about that. In any traditional school, you'll see students conversing, squabbling, working as a team and competing. You don't need to go to a forest to do those things.

I do wonder what would happen to those children who go to wilderness schools when they grow up and enter the workplace. Would they really be able to cope sitting in an office? What happens when the pressure is on – can they walk out of the office and go the woods for a week? Of course not. 10

Wilderness schools sound cool, but the practicalities are a problem. The outdoors can be a dangerous place. Will staff need expert training? How much will insurance cost? Who will be held accountable when accidents happen? Give me a normal school, normal exams and normal buildings. It's much easier.

Question 2

a Re-read this extract from Text C:

> 'As I say, I enjoyed school, but there were times when the pressure got a bit much. That's when nature saved me. There's a lot to be said for escaping into nature – into the wildlife. Spending time in the wilderness is calming. It takes you away from the demands of life and invites you to slow down and take in the world around you. Once you're free of the madness of modern life, you relax and take pleasure in simplicity. In short, you gain perspective – you come to realise that some of the things we get obsessed about are trivial.'

Use your own words to evaluate the writer's views on nature. Give details from the text to justify your answer. [5]

b Write an article for your local paper arguing your view on outdoor learning.

Use your own words to write your article based on what you have read in both Text C and Text D.

In your article you should:

- outline attitudes to outdoor learning

- explain some of the challenges outdoor schools would face.

Write about 250–350 words.

Up to 10 marks are available for reading and up to 25 marks for writing. [35]

Example student response	Examiner comments
2a The writer has some highly positive and emotionally charged views about nature. He positions nature as a contrast to school, depicting it as something that 'saved me'. This shows the writer's dramatic and heartfelt view of nature as something existential. He presents nature as a place of almost spiritual retreat that heals humans – it's 'calming' and 'invites you to slow down'. The writer sees natures as a restorative – an antidote to 'the madness of life'. His views on nature are wholly positive to the point where they seem a little melodramatic.	This response provides a detailed and thoughtful overview on the writer's view of nature. The student evaluates these views, judging the use of contrast and their heartfelt, existential qualities. The student also sees that the overwhelming positivity might be judged as slightly overdone. 5/5 marks

Example student response	Examiner comments
2b	This is a very well-written response that uses ambitious words, punctuation and sentence structures in an accurate way. It seamlessly echoes the ideas of the source texts and begins to build an argument.
The best of both worlds	
Educationalists often find themselves in polarising disputes. The latest overheated debates concern the advent of wilderness schools: those outdoor places of learning away from the confines of the classroom. Adherents of wilderness schools will tell you that they will help socialise your children; they will provide a place where children can happily learn, free of the strictures of traditional schools.	However, the argument falters and seems incomplete. The fourth paragraph signals the start of the student's argument but comes to an abrupt halt, possibly because the students has run out of time, or ideas. The response is also below the minimum word count.
And just as simplistically, opponents of wilderness schools will tell you these places will produce a generation of damaged adults who run out of offices when it all gets too much. They point to the practical problems of learning in the great outdoors – the insurance costs, the staff training, and the danger lurking around every tree.	A more successful answer would have a fully formed argument and should meet the minimum word count. 27/35 marks Reading: 7/10 marks Writing: 20/25 marks
As with most of these educational battles, the answer lies somewhere in the middle: it is possible, with careful planning, to integrate the benefits of the natural world in the classroom. It is beneficial to encourage young people to seek inner peace from nature; it is desirable to help students gain traditional qualifications that they will need for the world of work. But this takes thought.	
A good start would be to ensure every school had outdoor access. There are some inner city schools that only offer children concrete and glass – no space to explore nature. This must change.	

9 Descriptive writing

In this unit, you will practise the skills required to write effective descriptions. You will learn what the command word 'describe' means in the context of exam-style questions. You will explore how effective answers create atmosphere, and how they are structured to maintain the reader's interest. There are opportunities to use figurative language, sensory description and language choices to enliven your writing, and to practise using different points of view. You will test all of these skills in the context of exam-style questions.

9.1 Describing places

Descriptive tasks usually include the command word 'describe', or a specific instruction to 'Write a description'. This means you need to write about the characteristics and main features of the place, person, object or feeling given in the task.

An exam task that asks you to describe a place will state a general location – for example, a marketplace, a playground or an old building. Here, the command word 'describe' is a cue to show how well you can use language to convey the features of that location. A well-rounded description will also create a sense of atmosphere and emotion connected to that place, such as wonder, joy or calm.

1 Look at this writing task:

> Describe a memorable place you have visited.

a Look closely at the words in the question. If you were writing a response to this task, how would you interpret the word 'memorable'? For example, is the place you are thinking of memorable because it was beautiful, mysterious or scary?

b Write a plan for a response to this task. Include notes about the atmosphere or emotion you want to create.

Here is an example of a student's plan for Activity 1. Notice how the plan focuses on feelings and how this inspires some of the details that will be included in the descriptive piece.

> A description of a beach when the sun is setting. Create a feeling of beauty and peace as the day comes to an end. Focus on the majesty of the setting sun and the relaxed nature of the people watching the sun set.

You should not include lots of events in descriptive writing. However, it is important that something happens, to create a sense of movement or change and prevent your writing turning into a list of sense descriptions. This should not become a story. Keep the focus on atmosphere and detail. For example, you could shift between times of day, show a change in weather, or introduce something new into the scene. In the sample plan for the descriptive piece about the 'memorable place' (a beach) the student might include the following notes to build in a sense of change and extend the ideas:

> Describe the moment as the sun starts to go down through to the moment when it sets properly. Contrast the sights before and after.

2 Write a plan for the following task. Include ideas on what will happen to give your description a sense of movement.

> Describe an exciting place. It could be somewhere you have been to or an imagined place.

TIP

In an exam, spend five to ten minutes planning your writing. In that time, consider several possible atmospheres that might work before you decide which one to pursue. For example, writing about a busy beach in extreme temperatures would create a different atmosphere from writing about a deserted beach. You can also open up different ideas if you imagine a place at different times of the day or year, or when the location is busy or deserted.

> **TIP**
>
> When completing practice questions, always make a plan first and ensure it includes ideas for atmosphere and movement. There are different ways to set out a plan, so choose the way that best suits you. For example, you might make brief notes in sentence form, as in the examples here, or you could make a bullet-point list of ideas, or perhaps a mind map.

Remember that, unlike reading comprehension questions, composition questions are only brief prompts. You have a broad scope and only one task to complete. This means that underlying everything is your ability to be creative in timed conditions – to think of interesting ideas and details for your writing. The best way to develop this skill is to read widely for inspiration, use this book to try out the core skills, and then practise completing exam tasks in timed conditions.

3   Write about 350–450 words on the following question.

Up to 16 marks are available for the content and structure of your answer and up to 24 marks for the style and accuracy of your writing.

Describe a place you are very familiar with.   [40]

Good descriptive responses contain effective figurative language such as metaphor, simile and personification. These techniques show key writing skills and are very useful for creating different effects.

> **« RECALL AND CONNECT 1 «**
>
> What are the differences between metaphor, simile and personification? Write an example of each.

> **UNDERSTAND THESE TERMS**
>
> * metaphor
> * simile
> * personification

Look at this example of part of a good, descriptive response in which figurative language creates a peaceful atmosphere. Notice how the hills are described as if they are powerful and confident, like a benign ruler. The plane is also described using figurative language, as if it were a bee, and making its trails seem like a performance.

> The hills sat serenely, their green majesty confidently gazing over the valley below. Summer was here. The birds and insects busied themselves happily and somewhere high overhead, a small plane buzzed in circles, white trails dancing behind it.

4   Write a short paragraph describing a storm. Use some figurative language.

5   Write about 350–450 words on the following question.

Up to 16 marks are available for the content and structure of your answer and up to 24 marks for the style and accuracy of your writing.

Describe an outdoor scene.   [40]

TIP

Remember that the more you read, the more skilled you become at writing. Take time to read as many descriptive pieces as you can in a variety of styles and about different places, events and people. Take inspiration from published writers.

REFLECTION

How confident did you feel when using figurative language in your description? What were the challenges? How could you improve this aspect of your composition writing? Is there anything you would change about your approach to using figurative language next time you write?

6 Write about 350 to 450 words on the following question.

Up to 16 marks are available for the content and structure of your answer and up to 24 marks for the style and accuracy of your writing.

Describe a busy town centre.   [40]

9.2 Describing details

An effective response to a descriptive task will always include well-chosen details to bring your writing to life and provide information to help your readers picture the scene. You will decide on some of these details while you are planning your response, but some will occur to you as you write.

1 Read the following paragraph from an example student response.
It describes someone driving down a bank next to the sea.

> I took a left turn down Tyne Bank. Tall, spiked railings held back overgrown trees on both sides. They were the shadowy guards. The road soon narrowed, passing boarded-up garages. Sea birds whined overhead. Beyond the garages, on the left, was the dock where the furtive sea pulsed. The light was dying – a final net of gold on the water.

Write down examples of:

a figurative language used to describe the buildings and scenery

b interesting word choices to describe details.

To use details effectively in your descriptive writing you need to select the most appropriate and engaging words to convey the scene or describe the object. In the example above, the adjectives 'spiked', 'shadowy' and 'furtive' add detail to the nouns and help to convey a particular atmosphere.

2 Read the following paragraph from another example response.
It describes a journey to a small town using different adjectives.

> Soon, the lofty houses thinned out, and the sides of the road became greener. I rounded the tight bend by the remains of an old farm. A rusting, crimson tractor sat idle in the field. The road was a series of dramatic crests that revealed a view of the distant, purple mountains against the open sky. I looked left into the sleepy valley where Stockford nestled. Hunched houses and livestock were dotted along the river.

Create a table with three columns – Size, Colour and Qualities – and list all the adjectives in the paragraph in the correct column.

TIP

It is important to use words accurately, otherwise it will undermine the effect of your description. Make it part of your revision strategy to learn some effective words and practise using them correctly in context.

TIP

Remember that pairs of adjectives can be used to add detail. Use this technique sparingly in your writing – a well-chosen adjective is better than two less effective ones.

3 Read the following description of an airport. Rewrite it, adding some well-chosen adjectives to bring the scene to life.

> A taxi arrived at the drop-off point just outside the entrance to the airport. A family of four got out of the taxi. They were dressed in shorts and T-shirts and were excited for their holiday. At the other end of the airport, a cleaner made his way around the concourse. He cleared rubbish from the bins and swept the floor. It was a hot day, and the glass windows made the airport very warm. Travellers were fanning themselves as they stood in the queues to check in. The airport workers behind the desks were busy.

4 Write about 350–450 words on the following question.

Up to 16 marks are available for the content and structure of your answer and up to 24 marks for the style and accuracy of your writing.

Describe a scene featuring a sea or lake. [40]

5 Make a plan for the following task:

> Describe walking through a busy train station.

In your plan you should note:

- the overall atmosphere you are trying to create
- a list of things you would include
- an idea for how the scene might change.

6 Look at your plan from Activity 5. Choose two things you decided to include (second bullet point) and note down what specific details you could add to bring these things to life. Remember that the smaller details of colour, size and other qualities help your reader to picture what you are describing. Think about the precise words you could use to describe these things.

7 Write about 350–450 words on the following question.

Up to 16 marks are available for the content and structure of your answer and up to 24 marks for the style and accuracy of your writing.

Describe walking through a busy train station. [40]

Checking and editing your work is an important part of the process. In timed conditions, you will not be able to make any big structural changes, but you should always check that your writing is clear and makes sense, and that punctuation and spelling are accurate.

8 Read your response to Activity 7. Spend five minutes reading through your response. Check that each sentence makes clear sense and that punctuation is accurate. Identify any possible misspellings. If you are able to, correct these yourself. If not, use a dictionary to do so.

TIP

You will not be allowed to use a dictionary in an exam, but after you have attempted an exam-style question in this book, it is good practice to check and correct any misspellings.

REFLECTION

What helped you most when improving your use of details – reading the work of other writers or writing and editing your own work? Going forward, how could you continue to make improvements in how you include interesting details in your descriptive writing?

≪ RECALL AND CONNECT 2 ≪

Write down some reminders about ways to check your work and how you should divide your time in a descriptive writing task.

9   Write about 350–450 words on the following question.

Up to 16 marks are available for the content and structure of your answer and up to 24 marks for the style and accuracy of your writing.

Describe the final day of school before a holiday begins.   [40]

9.3 Using the senses

You have seen how the command word 'describe' is asking you to use language in a way that allows your reader to imagine the scene you are writing about. A key skill underpinning this is the use of sensory description. Humans experience the world through their senses, so a successful response to a descriptive task will employ sensory references.

≪ RECALL AND CONNECT 3 ≪

Remind yourself of the five senses, then write five sentences, each containing a different sensory description. You could focus all five sentences on the same scene – perhaps describing a busy café.

1   Read the following paragraph from an example response. The narrator describes entering an old, abandoned house. List all the references to sight, sound and touch in the response.

I slowly push open the wooden door, its paint flaked and blistered. The door feels rough and damp. It scrapes and squeals against the floor, the hinges croaking. As it opens fully, light is shed on the long, dark hallway. There are green tiles on the floor, some broken. My footsteps echo on these tiles; some of them crunch beneath my feet. I reach for the cold, plastic light switch. A dim, milky light is thrown across the hallway, causing old pictures to glare at me from the walls.

2   Make some notes on how you could continue the description from Activity 1, to describe walking up the stairs to another room. List what you might see, hear and touch. Then write a paragraph based on your notes. The paragraph should:

- contain sensory references
- use interesting words and figurative language
- be around 100 words.

3   Write about 350–450 words on the following question.

Up to 16 marks are available for the content and structure of your answer and up to 24 marks for the style and accuracy of your writing.

Describe attending a large family meal.   [40]

In Topic 9.1, you explored the importance of having something happen in your descriptive writing, to create a sense of movement or change. Any type of minor event makes your writing more interesting in both structure and content and will prevent it reading like a list of sense descriptions. In an exam response of 350–450 words, it can be a useful guide to have this moment of change roughly half-way through. This will give you space to describe the situation before and after the change.

4   Write down some suggestions for moments of change if you were writing a description of each of the following:

a   sitting on a sunny beach

b   walking through a beautiful garden

c   watching a bird or animal.

5   Write about 350–450 words on **one** of the following questions.

Up to 16 marks are available for the content and structure of your answer and up to 24 marks for the style and accuracy of your writing.

a   Describe sitting on a sunny beach.   [40]

b   Describe walking through a beautiful garden.   [40]

c   Describe watching a bird or animal.   [40]

Some exam tasks specifically ask you to write about a place at different moments in time. For example, you might be asked to describe a school early in the morning before students arrive and then at lunchtime. This allows you to show your skills at using sensory and figurative language to create different atmospheres or feelings in each part of your response.

6   Make a plan for the following task. Include ideas for sensory language you could include.

> Imagine a place you know well. Write a description of the place as it was in the past and as it is now.

In a similar way, you could be asked to describe a place or an object and your feelings about it. There are no rules about how many words you should write for each aspect of a task like this, but you must make sure you cover both aspects of the task – place/object and feelings.

> **TIP**
>
> Using figurative language to describe sensory experiences can be very effective. For example, describing the sound of hinges 'croaking' not only conveys their sound, but also suggests they are old and contributes to a sinister atmosphere.

> **TIP**
>
> It may be tempting to end your response at the exact moment a change occurs, but it is often more effective to show your reader how a change affects the scene – contrast can be a dramatic technique.

7 Plan a response to the following task.

> Describe a place of natural beauty and your feelings about it.

In your plan, you should include:

- the name of the place

- details about the place (sensory information)

- ideas for words, phrases and figurative language

- the overall effect you wish to create – the feeling it inspires in you.

8 Read this example paragraph from a response to the task in Activity 7, which describes Dinosaur Provincial Park in Canada. Identify:

a examples of words and sentences where the writer's feelings about the park come through strongly

b what you felt were the most effective descriptions.

> The twisted spires of sandstone stand proud, mesmerising monuments to long ago. I touch the base of these gritty pillars and marvel at their connection to the past. I close my eyes and listen to the light whistle of wind moving through the cacti, through the bristles, through the canyon. It's a sound of time past. In this alien land, my pulse beats in rhythm with the ancient world.

9 Write about 350–450 words on the following question.

Up to 16 marks are available for the content and structure of your answer and up to 24 marks for the style and accuracy of your writing.

Describe visiting a place that made you feel fearful. [40]

> **TIP**
>
> Some descriptive tasks might invite you to write about a place or situation you are familiar with. Some of the most effective descriptive writing is drawn from real experiences you have had and places you know, but you may find it helps to fictionalise some aspects of these experiences – inventing details for interest and variety.

9.4 Describing events

If an exam task asks you to describe an event, it will usually give you a prompt that sets up the basic details. However, you should spend some of your planning time deciding on the precise details of the event in order to bring it to life. Remember that this is still a descriptive task – you should not write a narrative response where you tell a story. Instead, focus on the details and feelings associated with the event.

1 Look at this task:

> Describe the discovery of an unusual object.

a What do the words 'discovery', 'unusual' and 'object' imply?

b Write down some ideas that you could use in a response to this task. Try to think of three different objects that you could describe in an interesting way.

2 Choose one of the objects you considered in Activity 1 and plan a response to the task. Include:

- where and how the object is discovered
- the feeling created when the object is discovered
- how your response would begin
- how your response would end.

3 Think about the smaller details of your response – what specific things might you include? Add to your plan with details about:

- the setting where the object is found
- the appearance of the object
- words you might use to describe it
- figurative language that would bring the object and its discovery to life.

> **TIP**
>
> Planning a piece of writing can feel time-consuming but remember that you should not spend too much time on your plan when writing in timed conditions. If you practise making plans for descriptive writing pieces using exam-style tasks, you will find that you will get quicker and can come up with creative ideas in a short amount of time.

Throughout the course, you will have practised writing from different points of view (the type of narrator used to tell a story) and expressing different perspectives (the narrator's feelings and attitudes). In an exam task, the question might specify a point of view. For example, if it includes the word 'you', it is probably best to write your description in the first person, as if you are seeing the place or experiencing the event you are describing through the narrator's eyes. However, many exam tasks will leave the point of view up to you. As part of the planning phase, you will need to decide which one best suits the response you want to write.

> **TIP**
>
> There are benefits to both first- and third-person points of view. Writing in the third person could mean that your narrator is omniscient – they can see anything. First person has the benefit of being very close to the action, so it allows you greater access to the narrator's thoughts and feelings.

4 Write a plan for each of the following tasks, spending a maximum of five minutes on each plan. Include some specific details that you would include in a full response. Think carefully which point of view might be most effective for each task.

a Describe losing a valuable object.

b Describe two old friends meeting after they have not seen each other for a long time.

c Describe a minor accident.

> **TIP**
>
> The structure of an event-based description can be straightforward – the first part might focus on the moments before an event happens and the second part on the moments afterwards. However, you can also use more interesting structures. For example, you could start at the moment of discovery.

> **UNDERSTAND THESE TERMS**
>
> - point of view
> - perspective
> - first person
> - third person
> - omniscient

How easy or difficult did you find it to plan the details for these tasks in timed conditions? Why do you think that was? Which elements of planning do you need to practise more:

- keeping to a five-minute limit

- coming up with creative ideas under pressure

- noting down your ideas clearly

- putting your ideas in the best order

- deciding on an effective opening?

5 Write about 350–450 words on the following question.

Up to 16 marks are available for the content and structure of your answer and up to 24 marks for the style and accuracy of your writing.

Describe receiving an unusual object. [40]

To learn how to write a good composition, read as many examples of good responses to descriptive tasks as you can. As you do so, take the time to really think about why the response is effective. Start by considering the core idea of the response – the way in which the student has taken the basic prompt in the task and decided on the larger elements of their response. For the task in Activity 5, for example, this might be what the unusual object is and how it arrives. Then look at the smaller details included in the response, such as figurative language, sense impressions, language and grammatical choices.

6 Read the following paragraph from an example response to Activity 5. Make notes on the following:

a how engaging you found the idea

b how sense impressions are used to describe the event

c the most effective word choices used.

> Kareem turned over the envelope once again. It was old and yellowing, the paper coarse against his fingers. He recognised the spidery writing from somewhere – the angular, blue flourishes and dots. Kareem placed the envelope on his desk and switched on the lamp. Stark white lit up the envelope, and through the thinness of the paper; he could see an outline of an object. His fingers traced the object. It was small and metallic. He slid his finger under the flap of the envelope and carefully teased it open. His fingers slowly delved into the envelope and lifted it out. There, gleaming in the light, was a small, golden ring.

There are several effective ways to begin a piece of descriptive writing. For example, you could focus on:

- a specific place

- the weather

- scenery

- touch

- feelings.

7 The opening of the example response in Activity 6 begins by focusing on the sense of touch. Rewrite the opening by focusing on a different aspect.

8 Write a 200-word response to the task in Activity 1:

> Describe the discovery of an unusual object.

You can base it on the plans you made in previous activities or a different idea. Remember to:

- decide what point of view you will write from

- use sensory description

- include engaging details

- use figurative language

- take care with word choices, phrasing and spelling.

9 Write about 350–450 words on the following question.

Up to 16 marks are available for the content and structure of your answer and up to 24 marks for the style and accuracy of your writing.

Describe being given an unexpected gift. [40]

9.5 Describing people

As well as places, objects and feelings, you could also be asked to describe a person. This may invite you to describe someone you know, such as a friend or a family member, or you may be asked to describe a fictional character in a situation given in the prompt. When describing a person, whether real or imagined, you should not just describe their appearance – you need to describe their personality and manner, too.

> **TIP**
>
> Remember – 'show, don't tell'. Do not give direct information about a character but rather show what they are like through their actions and dialogue.

1 Read the following character outline.

Mo is a 25-year-old man. He enjoys going to the gym, has an expensive car and is a little arrogant.

Write a paragraph describing Mo. Rather than just stating facts, find a way to show these characteristics.

2 Read the following descriptive paragraph about Mo. Identify how the writer has used:

   a ways to show Mo's appearance

   b situations to show Mo's personality.

> Mo studied his biceps in the mirror, examining their contours and size, a broad smile playing across his lips. He glanced at his face, checked his stubble, and thought how his new haircut suited him perfectly — how it accentuated his coral blue eyes. In the mirror, he could see his sports car parked outside the gym window, its metallic red bodywork gleaming in the sun. Soon, he'd see just how fast it could go.

In real life, you learn a lot about people by how they react to different situations. In a similar way, placing someone in different situations in your writing can reveal various aspects of their character. Take care to choose the most revealing verbs to convey how your character speaks, moves and behaves.

3 What might each of the following situations reveal about the character of Mo?

   a An older lady asks Mo to help her carry some shopping to her car.

   b Mo is about to start a new job, working for a powerful man that he is desperate to impress.

4 Write a paragraph describing Mo walking towards his expensive car, climbing in and driving away. Focus on choosing effective verbs to convey Mo's personality.

5 Write about 350–450 words on the following question.

Up to 16 marks are available for the content and structure of your answer and up to 24 marks for the style and accuracy of your writing.

Describe a person acting suspiciously. [40]

Character-based descriptive exam tasks may ask you to write about contexts or situations that you are familiar with. Remember that you can describe something from your own experience if you think that would make a good response to the task, but just because you have personal experience of a situation, you do not have to write about that experience – you can invent one. Most writers blend aspects of their own experiences with fictional ones.

6 Make a plan for the following task.

> Describe a teenage student on their first day at a new school.

In your plan, include ideas about:

- the overall atmosphere of the description
- how the student feels
- how you will convey the student's feelings
- what point of view you will write in
- how the piece will begin, develop and end.

REFLECTION

Do you feel you are getting better at planning a piece of descriptive writing in timed conditions? Why, or why not? What could you still do to improve your planning techniques, especially in terms of working efficiently to a time limit?

7   Develop your plan from Activity 6 by focusing on the smaller ideas and details. Note down some ideas about:

   • specific aspects of the student and the school

   • ideas for figurative language and word choices.

8   Write about 350–450 words on the following question.

   Up to 16 marks are available for the content and structure of your answer and up to 24 marks for the style and accuracy of your writing.

   Describe a student leaving school for the last time.   [40]

Exam tasks that ask you to describe someone you know offer a slightly different challenge. These tasks may feel personal so your writing may end up more like an account than a descriptive piece – you could mistakenly 'tell, rather than show'. So, if you choose to write about someone you know, be extra careful to use interesting words, figurative language and varied sentences to convey the person.

The prompts for tasks about familiar people may invite you to justify some aspect of their relationship to you.

9   Make a plan for the following exam task.

   Describe a family member who is important to you.

   Your plan should include details of:

   • who the person is

   • why they are important to you

   • specific details about their manner and appearance.

10 Think further about the important family member from Activity 9. Think of:

   • a situation you could place them in – an act or experience that shows their character

   • ways you could use figurative language and interesting language choices in your description.

TIP

When writing about real people it is still important to use language in interesting ways – rather than writing in a factual style. Be inventive with words and phrases and use figurative language. Remember – you are trying to show the quality of your writing.

11   Write about 350–450 words on **one** of the following questions.

Up to 16 marks are available for the content and structure of your answer and up to 24 marks for the style and accuracy of your writing.

a   Describe a character in a dangerous situation.   [40]

b   Describe a family member who you are particularly close to.   [40]

9.6 Improving descriptive writing

Getting better at writing is a journey. You should see your exam preparation period as a chance to refine and perfect your work. Often, changing major structural aspects of your work is a good way to improve your work, but in an exam, you will not always have the time to do this. You should, however, set aside time in an exam to check and amend your work where necessary.

The effectiveness of a piece of descriptive writing is partly determined by accuracy – how good your spelling, punctuation and grammar are. It can be difficult to write flawless English in timed conditions, but examiners are aware that you are writing in a pressurised situation. However, you should always leave time at the end to check your writing as carefully as possible and fix any errors.

1   Make a list of the different types of errors you might check for when you have finished writing a response to a descriptive task.

2   Make a note of some common errors you have made in your writing. These might be spelling or grammar errors. Note down some ways you have or could overcome these errors.

> **REFLECTION**
>
> What methods have you used to identify errors you make? How do you ensure that you avoid making these errors more than once? What could help you improve the technical aspects of your writing?

3   Read the following paragraph from an example response. The task was to describe a character in a dangerous situation, and the student chose to describe a scenario in which they are walking in extreme heat. This is the final paragraph in the response.

The sun was still beating down on me from above. I was almost home. Soon, I'd rest, drink lots of water and sit in the shade. I wiped the sweat from my hat, put it back on my head and walked on. The ground was parched beneath my feet, but every step took me closer to home. My muscles ached and my mouth was very dry. I thought about getting home. I couldn't wait. Suddenly, I turned the corner, walked into my house, got some water and sat down.

The response is competent but lacks interest. Note down three ways you could improve it, then rewrite the paragraph. Write around 100 words.

4 Look back at the full writing tasks you have completed in this unit. Choose one of them and write notes on ways you could improve it as a piece of writing. You might consider the quality of:

- your initial idea
- the structure of your response
- the ending
- your choice of phrasing
- word choices and figurative language
- accuracy of spelling, punctuation and grammar.

5 Rewrite the response you identified in the previous activity to make it more effective.

6 Write about 350–450 words on the following question.

Up to 16 marks are available for the content and structure of your answer and up to 24 marks for the style and accuracy of your writing.

Describe a situation when you felt nervous. [40]

SELF-ASSESSMENT CHECKLIST

Let's revisit the learning objectives for this unit.
Decide how confident you are with each statement.

Now I can	Show it	Needs more work	Almost there	Confident to move on
plan ideas for descriptive writing	Write a plan for the following task which includes the overall atmosphere you are trying to create: Describe visiting a deserted town.			
use figurative language to describe places, events and people	Write a short paragraph in which you use two examples of figurative language to describe a deserted town.			
use sensory descriptions to develop the content of my writing	Write a short paragraph describing being caught in a rainstorm. Use effective sensory description.			
use different points of view and perspectives	Look back at one of your responses in this unit and write a brief explanation of why you chose a particular point of view.			

CONTINUED

Now I can	Show it	Needs more work	Almost there	Confident to move on
write engaging openings and endings	Look back at one of your exam-style responses in this unit and write a brief explanation showing how you have tried to create an engaging opening and ending.			
make effective language choices	Write a short paragraph describing the moment when a person arrives home. Use a range of effective adjectives and verbs.			
practise accurate use of spelling, punctuation and grammar.	Look back at your exam-style responses in this unit and identify specific places where you have corrected spelling, punctuation and grammar to make it accurate.			

10 Narrative writing

SKILLS FOCUS

In this unit you will:

- generate story ideas and write plans

- create engaging characters and settings

- write effective story openings and endings

- structure narratives in different ways

- use a range of language techniques to engage the reader

- practise accurate use of spelling, punctuation and grammar.

EXAM SKILLS FOCUS

In this unit you will:

- understand what is meant by the command in an exam task to 'write a story'

- practise writing a response in timed conditions

- understand what a good answer looks like.

Throughout your English studies, you will have had many opportunities to develop your narrative writing skills. When you write a story in exam conditions, you are expected to demonstrate these skills under the pressure of time. This unit will reinforce your understanding of areas such as planning, developing characters, and writing effective openings and endings. It will also help you to practise applying these skills in timed conditions using exam-style tasks.

10.1 Story elements and ideas

UNDERSTAND THESE TERMS

- story
- narrative

Many of the skills you practised in descriptive writing, such as planning, structuring and phrasing, also apply to narrative writing. However, when you choose a narrative rather than a descriptive task in the exam, you will need to write about a sequence of events. Most narrative tasks ask you to 'write a story', which means producing a piece of writing that contains a series of events that happen to a character – a tale with a beginning, some development and an ending.

You will not have time to plan every detail of a story in exam conditions; you will have to decide on some smaller details and aspects of language as you write. However, you should map out the broader structural aspects of your narrative at the start. For example:

- What could the conflict in the story be?
- Who is the main character?
- What will happen to the character – how will the conflict develop?
- What will happen to the character at the end of the story?

> **TIP**
>
> Remember that stories are driven by conflict – a challenge that a character has to overcome. These conflicts might be other people, situations or the characters' own feelings.

1   Write a plan for the following task using the prompts above.

> Write a story that begins with the words, 'As I left the house, I felt incredibly nervous.'

2   Read the following example plan for the task in Activity 1. Make notes on any areas that you think might benefit from improvement. Which of the ideas seem least effective and why?

Conflict: The character is about to start a new school – they are nervous about meeting new people.

Main character: A young man who has moved from a rural area to a busy city with his family.

What happens: The character worries as he walks to school; he feels isolated. When he arrives, there is no one to talk to. Then he meets someone at break time – a friendly person who is welcoming. They spend some of the day chatting and over the next few weeks become good friends. They visit each other's houses and during the year, do lots of interesting things together.

How it ends: The character feels much happier by the end of the year.

The word count for a composition task is 350–450 words, so you need to keep the action focused. Do not include more than one or two main characters in more than one or two settings, and do not try to cover a long period of time.

3   Rewrite the third point in the plan in Activity 2 to make the action more compact instead of being spread over a whole school year.

Planning under the pressure of time is one of the main challenges of writing in exam conditions. Remember that you should only spend five to ten minutes planning your composition, so practise creating plans for stories with a timer on. Within that time, try to think of a few options for potential characters, settings and conflicts. Sometimes your first idea is the best, but often playing around with different ideas can have good results.

4   Write a plan for the following task. Do not spend more than ten minutes on your plan.

> Write a story that begins with the words, 'She was unaware that her life was about to change forever.'

TIP

The more you read, the more ideas you will have to draw on when it comes to planning your own narratives. Read a variety of writers and genres to gain a wide variety of ideas.

REFLECTION

Which part of the planning did you find most challenging – coming up with the initial idea? Thinking of a character? Deciding a sequence of events? Why do you think that is? How might you refine your planning skills?

Narrative writing should develop the story around some kind of conflict. A conflict may be between two characters – a protagonist and an antagonist – but there are other types of conflict, too. If the stakes are not high enough in the conflict, the story will be less effective. For example, a story about a man going home from work could be very dull indeed, but if the man must get home quickly to receive a very important delivery, then that adds some drama. This becomes even more effective is there is something preventing him from doing so – a traffic jam, for instance.

5   Write about 350–450 words on the following question.

Up to 16 marks are available for the content and structure of your answer and up to 24 marks for the style and accuracy of your writing.

Write a story that begins with the words, 'The door opened, and I couldn't believe what I saw.'   [40]

UNDERSTAND THESE TERMS

*   protagonist
*   antagonist

Always consider whether the problem your character faces in the narrative could be intensified. Find ways to make the character's experience more compelling for the reader – something very engaging. Ask yourself whether your reader will be emotionally gripped by the conflict. For example, a sample response to Activity 5, might be very compelling if the narrator opens the door to find a wounded animal that needs urgent care. This idea might stimulate the reader's emotions. It would be further increased if the animal was potentially dangerous.

6   Re-read your response to Activity 5. Write down some ideas for how you could make the conflict more compelling.

7   Write about 350 to 450 words on the following question.

Up to 16 marks are available for the content and structure of your answer and up to 24 marks for the style and accuracy of your writing.

Write a story with the title, 'The storm'.   [40]

10.2 Story openings

As you have seen, some narrative tasks provide you with an opening sentence and invite you to continue a story from that point. This gives you a helpful starting point – a suggestion of a situation – but you will still need to carefully build an opening section that engages your reader's interest and gets the story underway.

The opening section of your narrative should:

- introduce the character and/or situation

- give a sense of the setting

- quickly establish an event or hook to make the reader want to continue reading.

1   Read the following example opening paragraph to a narrative entitled 'The door'.

> The sky threatened as I made my way along the road. It looked like a thin black tongue of fresh-looking tarmac. No road markings. A metal gate was tied open, bound to a concrete post with a thick piece of nylon rope. I entered slowly, bumping over potholes, and parked. Forklift trucks sat awkwardly on the compound in front of a vast and solemn warehouse. The main part of the building was windowless. At the front, there was a reception area, which looked like an afterthought, its sole window dark. Alongside it, a yellow metal door was slightly ajar, light at its edges. I was here.

   a   List the parts of the story that make you want to read on. Consider both the situation and the way it is described.

   b   Using examples, explain how figurative language is used here to help create a sense of intrigue.

A good way to hook your reader is to withhold information (keep details from them) right at the start. This can create a sense of mystery or get a reader wondering what the story is really about. The paragraph in Activity 1, for example, makes the reader want to know what is behind the door.

You can also withhold information by using the pronoun 'it', so the reader is not sure what you are referring to. However, make sure you eventually reveal or explain what 'it' is. For example, another sample response to the task in Activity 1 does this:

> Birds circled overhead as I reached for the handle. The hinges of the door had dropped, a groove cut in the stone floor. I dragged the door open and peered around. There it was. It was smaller than I expected, but just as valuable.

2   Write an opening paragraph in response to the following task. Write around 100 words. Set up the situation and character and use a hook to engage your reader's interest.

> Write a story with the title, 'The city'.

You only have 350–450 words in which to tell your story, so do not spend a long time setting the scene. You need to reach a moment of action by the end of the first paragraph. As part of your preparation for the exam, ensure you check the openings of stories you have written and make sure they get to the action quickly.

TIP

'Hooks' are designed to grab a reader's attention and make them want to find out what will happen. You should always include a hook in your opening paragraph. This will probably be related to the main conflict in the story, so think about events that will create a sense of mystery, wonder or fear for the character.

UNDERSTAND THIS TERM

- pronoun

3   Look again at your opening to the task in Activity 2. Which bits could you cut or tighten to make for a more effective opening?

4   Write about 350–450 words on the following question.

Up to 16 marks are available for the content and structure of your answer and up to 24 marks for the style and accuracy of your writing.

Write a story with the title, 'Alone'.   [40]

You do not have to wait until the end of the first paragraph to reach a moment of action. One effective opening technique is to drop the reader right in the middle of the action – *in media res*. This makes the reader want to read on to understand the situation. It also has the benefit of saving some precious words setting the scene. Try out this technique in Activity 5.

5   Write about 350–450 words on the following question.

Up to 16 marks are available for the content and structure of your answer and up to 24 marks for the style and accuracy of your writing.

Write a story with the title, 'Going home'.   [40]

≪ RECALL AND CONNECT 1 ≪

Write a definition of a simple, compound and complex sentence. Explain how using a variety of sentence types can help to create interest in your writing.

The higher bands in the writing mark scheme are partly concerned with varied sentence structures. The more sophisticated your use of different sentence types, the more of the 24 marks available for style and accuracy you are likely to get.

6   Rewrite the opening section of your response to Activity 5. Aim to improve the variety of sentences you have used. Consider where you might be able to place minor sentences alongside complex ones in order to achieve certain effects.

7   Write about 350–450 words on the following question.

Up to 16 marks are available for the content and structure of your answer and up to 24 marks for the style and accuracy of your writing.

Write a story that begins with the words, 'It was the strangest feeling in the world.'   [40]

10.3 Characterisation

Narrative writing focuses on things that happen to a character, and how that character reacts to them. An exam prompt may imply something about a character (such as their age), but often the details of a character will be left up to you.

Most main characters are sympathetic – that is, a reader likes them and hopes that things work out for them. Sympathetic characters display admirable qualities, such as kindness or fairness. Readers also engage with characters that find themselves in difficult situations.

UNDERSTAND THIS TERM

- *in media res*

TIP

It is a good idea to show your command of different sentence types early on in your response, to make it clear that you understand when each sentence type is appropriate and what effects they can have – on their own and in combination.

1 Read the following notes on a character that might appear in a piece of narrative writing.

Shania is a teenage girl who loves nature. She particularly likes birds and animals. Her parents are busy people, and she has several brothers and sisters, so she does not always get a lot of attention. Shania is polite and gets along well with people but also likes to spend time alone.

Make your own brief notes on how you could use Shania as the main character in a story based on the following tasks.

> Write a story that begins with the words, 'The path was long, but she continued walking.'

> Write a story with the title, 'A busy time'.

Although it is best to make your main character sympathetic, you should also give them a flaw or two – less admirable qualities – to make them more relatable.

2 Read the following example notes on a flawed character that might appear in a piece of narrative writing.

Kemi is an ambitious character. She is a young mother who wants the best for her children and is very supportive of them. She demands the very best from her children, but occasionally she can lose her temper.

Make your own brief notes on how you could use Kemi as the main character in a story based on the following tasks.

> Write a story that begins with the words, 'It had been a long day and there was still plenty left to do.'

> Write a story with the title, 'Family holiday'.

3 Write about 350 to 450 words on the following question.

Up to 16 marks are available for the content and structure of your answer and up to 24 marks for the style and accuracy of your writing.

Write a story that begins with the words, 'It was getting dark and there was still two hours to go.' [40]

Sometimes you will need to give the reader direct information about your character. However, most of the time your reader should learn about the character through how they behave, speak and respond to situations. In particular, you can reveal a lot about a character by placing them in a challenging situation.

> **TIP**
>
> As you prepare for your exam, compile notes and ideas about different characters that you might be able to use in a story. Include details about their age, personality, interests and relationships. If one of your prepared characters fits a prompt you are given in an exam, it will save you some planning time.

4   Read the following opening paragraph to a narrative entitled 'First day at a new job'. It tells the reader about the character rather than letting their words and actions reveal information about them. Rewrite this scene so Kara's character comes across more naturally.

It was Kara's first day at her new job. She was wearing a smart new business suit, new black shoes that were too tight, and she carried a leather bag. She felt nervous as she walked along. Kara was hurrying because she was late for the train.

Character is also conveyed through dialogue – not just what characters say, but how they say it. In a short piece of narrative writing, dialogue can be an efficient way to convey character. Use speech tags sparingly to show how characters speak.

TIP

Remember the rules for setting out dialogue:

* Put a new speaker on a new line.
* Put the words spoken inside speech marks.
* Capitalise the first letter inside the speech marks.
* Include a punctuation mark, such as a comma, full stop or exclamation mark, before the closing speech mark.

---

5   Try experimenting with a different way to open a story. Using the scenario in Activity 4, write some dialogue between Kara and her husband as Kara leaves the house for her first day in her new job. Try to convey:

* the situation (that Kara is going to her new job)
* that she feels nervous
* that her husband supports her.

TIP

Starting a story with dialogue can make for an interesting and imaginative opening, as it can reveal a character's feelings and situation, so practise doing this. Make sure your reader knows who is speaking by using speech tags where appropriate.

UNDERSTAND THESE TERMS

* dialogue
* speech tag
* narrative voice

Deciding which point of view to write in is an important choice. Some exam tasks may specifically direct you to write in first person – for example, 'Write a story about a time when you felt scared'. However, most exam tasks are flexible enough to allow you to choose a point of view. For example, a task inviting you to begin a story with the words 'Jannich was late again' might seem like an invitation to write in third-person narrative voice, yet it is possible that you could write a response to this task in the first person – you could start: 'Jannich was late again, but this was no surprise to me. After all, I'd spent most of my life waiting for him.'

6   Write a plan for the following task. As you do so, experiment with first- and third-person narrative voices.

> Write a story with the title, 'Running away'.

REFLECTION

Do you find it more comfortable to write stories in first or third person? Why?
Do you feel that either of these options is better suited to demonstrating writing skills in an exam? Why?

7   Write about 350 to 450 words on the following question.

Up to 16 marks are available for the content and structure of your answer and up to 24 marks for the style and accuracy of your writing.

Write a story that begins with the words, 'The lights in the village were going out.'   [40]

10.4 Improving narrative structure

Although the word count for a narrative in an exam is only 350–450 words, your story should still have a clear structure that reaches a satisfying end point. Make sure you consider the structure of your narrative in your five- to ten-minute planning time.

One element of story structure concerns how you handle time. Many stories are best told in chronological order, and in timed conditions with a limited word count this might be the best approach. However, you may decide to bring interest to your writing by including non-chronological aspects such as a flashforward.

1   Read the following paragraph from an example response to the following exam task:

> Write a story that begins with the words, 'The sky darkened, and the storm was let loose.'

Notice how the student has used a non-chronological opening, using the prompt as part of a brief flashforward.

The sky darkened, and the storm was let loose. The rain came down in torrents, soaking me to the skin. The day had started out much brighter – when I woke, the sun was poking insistently through the blinds, urging me to get out of bed. Today was an important day after all.

Write an opening paragraph to the following task, using a flashforward.

> Write a story with the title, 'The worst journey'.

UNDERSTAND THESE TERMS

- chronological
- non-chronological
- flashforward

It is a good idea to practise planning and writing the middle part of a story in timed conditions, as this can often be the most difficult part to get right. Remember that this section should increase tension, putting your main character under more pressure.

Look at this plan for a response to the task in Activity 1. Notice how points 2 and 3 increase the tension.

1   man needs to urgently visit an ageing relative.

2   The man sets off in his car, but a heavy storm causes traffic problems.

3   The man abandons his car and decides to run the last section of the journey, but the route is challenging, and time is running out.

4   The man makes it just in time.

2   Write a plan for the following task. Make sure that the middle section contains some type of increasing tension.

> Write a story with the title, 'Lost at sea'.

3   Write about 350–450 words on the following question.

Up to 16 marks are available for the content and structure of your answer and up to 24 marks for the style and accuracy of your writing.

Write a story that begins with the words, 'Nobody was prepared for his arrival.'   [40]

Remember the following common structure for narrative texts:

- Exposition
- Complication
- Climax
- Resolution.

When you write a story in timed conditions, you will need to decide how much time to spend writing each part of the narrative.

4   Look back at your response to Activity 3.

    a   Roughly how much time did you spend on each section?

    b   On reviewing your response, do you think it would be better to spend more or less time on certain sections? Why?

5   Make a plan for the following task under the headings of the four stages of a narrative. Think about how many paragraphs you might need for each section and note down roughly how much time you will spend writing each one. Spend five to ten minutes writing your plan.

> Write a story with the title, 'Coming home'.

Another way to think about the structure of a narrative is to consider the journey the main character will go on – what things will happen to them? What will they experience? This often means planning how a character overcomes a challenge, or how they learn or discover something by the end of the story.

6   Look at the plan you wrote in Activity 5. What journey has the character experienced by the end? Is there a sense that they have overcome or learnt something? If not, amend the plan to include these elements.

7   Write about 350–450 words on the following question.

Up to 16 marks are available for the content and structure of your answer and up to 24 marks for the style and accuracy of your writing.

Write a story that begins with the words, 'It was that time of the year again.'   [40]

> **REFLECTION**
>
> What structural patterns do you see in your own writing? Do you find any particular part of story-writing especially easy or difficult? Why do you think that is? Are there areas of a story that you need to refine? How will you do this?

10.5 Refining your storytelling

You might think that you cannot revise for a writing exam – there is no content to learn, after all, and no facts to commit to memory. However, you can refine and practise the skills you need to write well, so see each practice piece you write as an opportunity to reflect on and then develop those skills. Writing a short story under the pressure of time offers a different set of challenges, of course, so in this section, you will practise ways to develop skills in your preparation period, but also how to write effectively in timed conditions.

In your exam, you only have one hour to plan, write and check a story. This means you need to be strict with your timings and also make sensible decisions about your narrative. Remember that you should:

- focus on a dramatic or emotionally engaging moment
- quickly set up the problem or challenge
- establish the characters through their actions
- use dialogue sparingly, including it only when it really helps the story
- build tension to a climax.

1   Look at the following task:

> Write a story with the title, 'The end of the journey'.

Write a plan for the task in five minutes maximum. Then look at your plan again and decide if you could improve any elements. Think about:

- the engaging moment on which your story will focus

- how you can quickly set up the problem

- how you will build tension to a climax.

Successful narrative writing uses the features of fiction in a convincing way. Remember, it is about quality not quantity. The top of the mark scheme rewards effective climaxes, characterisation, description and a well-defined plot – not how much you have written in the time allowed. Always write to the specified word count – 350–450 words.

2   Look at the two example paragraphs from the climax section of two responses to the task in Activity 1. Why is Response 2 better than Response 1? Consider:

- the ways in which the climax is described

- the ways in which character is revealed

- the use of description

- the use of different sentence types.

Response 1

Pedro reached the top of the hill and looked down at the valley below. He could see his house. Pedro breathed a sigh of relief and started walking down the hill. He would be home soon and he was delighted about that.

Response 2

The sun was at its peak as Pedro reached the summit of the hill. His heart was beating faster now, not just because of the ascent, but because as he looked down into the valley, he could finally see it. There, nestled in the green valley among the dots of cattle and the meandering stream was a place he longed to be. Home.

3   Look back at the climactic moment in your response to the task in Activity 1. How might you improve the way character, description, word choices and sentences are used? Rewrite it, aiming to improve the emotional moment you are writing about.

4   Write about 350–450 words on the following question.

Up to 16 marks are available for the content and structure of your answer and up to 24 marks for the style and accuracy of your writing.

Write a story with the title, 'The climb'.   [40]

≪ RECALL AND CONNECT 2 ≪

What are the three stages of checking and correcting your work? Write a brief explanation of each stage.

Checking and editing your work in an exam situation is very different to doing so in a piece of classwork. When you redraft in class, you can make significant changes to structure and content – even rewrite sections of a story altogether. It is good to practice this ahead of the exam, as it will teach you what writing pitfalls to avoid and generally if there are better ways to approach your writing. In an exam, of course, you should only take about five minutes at the end to proofread and check your writing.

Make sure that your writing makes sense – that you have used language in a way that can be understood. Next, make any small alterations to spelling and punctuation. It is easy when you write in timed conditions to make small errors. If you find missing punctuation, add it. If you find a misspelling, put a line through the word and write the correct spelling above. Beyond that, you may alter some words if you feel it would make your work better. This can be as simple as selecting a more interesting synonym.

> **TIP**
>
> Examiners understand that it is difficult to write flawlessly in timed conditions. It is possible to receive full marks with some minor errors, so it is best to write interesting and ambitious English (even if you make slight mistakes), rather than writing dull but accurate stories.

5   Look back at your response to Activity 4. Spend five minutes making any adjustments you feel will improve your writing.

6   Write about 350–450 words on the following question.

Up to 16 marks are available for the content and structure of your answer and up to 24 marks for the style and accuracy of your writing.

Write a story that begins with the words, 'It was always a difficult time to visit.'   [40]

10.6 Endings

The ending of a story is where its meaning emerges – usually connected with the success or failure of the main character. Stories tend to end in one of three ways: happily (giving the reader a sense of closure), sadly or in an unresolved way. Examiners have no preference for which type of ending you use, but it is important that it is satisfying in some way – that it suits the story you have built. To make sure you achieve this, always include the ending in your plan so you can be sure it makes sense for the character and fits with the story you are going to tell. You may even find it helpful to plan the ending first and work backwards.

> **TIP**
>
> Unresolved endings, such as cliffhangers, or 'open' endings (where the conflict is not fully resolved) can be useful options in timed conditions.

UNDERSTAND THESE TERMS

- closure
- cliffhanger

In order to resolve a well-rounded storyline in 350–450 words, make sure the action of the story is tightly focused on a specific moment.

1   Write a plan for the following task. Focus the story on a specific moment and plan a satisfactory resolution.

> Write a story that begins with the words, 'I reached out in desperation.'

2 Write about 350–450 words on the following question.

Up to 16 marks are available for the content and structure of your answer and up to 24 marks for the style and accuracy of your writing.

Write a story that begins with the words, 'I reached out in desperation.'   [40]

The ending of your story – its resolution – should be quite compact. Long-drawn-out endings are rarely satisfying, so most stories end quite soon after the moment of climax.

3 Look at the following task and an example paragraph from the ending of two different responses. Which one is better? Note down some reasons why you think this.

> Write a story with the title, 'The end of the journey'.

Response 1

Peter opened the gate and walked up the path. He was finally home. He said hello to his wife and family and put his bag down. It had been a long journey, one that he never thought would come to an end, but now he was home. He sat down and told his family about his adventure. They were all pleased to see him. That night, Peter had a great sleep and when he woke up the next day, he felt totally refreshed.

Response 2

Peter opened the gate, hearing the familiar creak of the hinges, the one he hadn't heard for months. As he walked up the path, gravel crunching beneath his feet, it was as if his body was beginning to relax. He found that time was slowing down, and the expectant faces at the window were miles away. He walked the last few steps as the door opened. 'Daddy!' his son shouted. He was home.

4 Look again at your response to Activity 2, paying close attention to the climax and resolution. Rewrite these parts to make sure your resolution is brief and impactful.

5 In this unit, you have read advice about planning, writing and checking stories in exam conditions. Look back through every section in this unit and compile a list of this advice. Keep it handy to refer to as you prepare for the exam and use it to complete Activity 6.

6 Write about 350–450 words on the following question.

Up to 16 marks are available for the content and structure of your answer and up to 24 marks for the style and accuracy of your writing.

Write a story with the title, 'Last chance'.   [40]

SELF-ASSESSMENT CHECKLIST

Let's revisit the learning objectives for this unit.
Decide how confident you are with each statement.

Now I can	Show it	Needs more work	Almost there	Confident to move on
generate story ideas and write plans	Write a plan for the following task: Write a story with the title, 'The best day ever'.			
create engaging characters and settings	Look back at one of your responses in this unit and explain the ways in which you created an interesting character and setting.			
write effective story openings and endings	Write the opening and ending sections of a story prompted by the following task: Write a story with the title, 'No going back'.			
structure narratives in different ways	Look back at two of your responses in this unit and write a brief explanation of how you structured them and why.			
use a range of language techniques to engage the reader	Find three examples from your responses to tasks in this unit that show you have used language techniques and choices that would interest a reader.			
use spelling, punctuation and grammar accurately.	Look back at your exam-style responses in this unit and identify specific places where you have corrected spelling, punctuation and grammar to make it accurate.			

Exam practice 5

The practice questions in this section will allow you to demonstrate the skills you have covered in this unit and will help you prepare for the assessment.

The following questions have example student responses and commentaries. For each task, write your own response first, then compare your answer to the example student response and commentary. Read the commentaries carefully and see whether any of the comments apply to your response also. Use the examiner commentaries to consider how you could improve your response.

Question 1

1   Write about 350–450 words on the following question.

Up to 16 marks are available for the content and structure of your answer and up to 24 marks for the style and accuracy of your writing.

Describe being in a strange room.   [40]

Example student response	Examiner comments
The room is verry warm but dark. I can see nothing apart from a warderobe and light around the edge of the curtains.	This response is focused on the task. It describes a room, as the task requires, and focuses on sights, sounds and feelings.
I can hear birds singing outside. I remember arriving late last night and being so tired that I went straight to bed – not even unpacking my suitcase. The last thing I can remember was staring at the ceiling before going to sleep. Now I'm awake but I can't find my glasses.	The spelling and punctuation are mainly accurate, but there are some errors. Sometimes commas are used instead of full stops, and there are random capital letters in places, and the occasional misspelling (e.g. 'verry' and 'tiried').
The room is too warm, the heating has been on all night, and I can feel like I'm trapped in a boiling hot cave.	The response is repetitive at times with several references to the wardrobe, curtains and birds. These might work better if these things had a sense of movement or development.
I want to get up, but I'm still tiried from yesterday, I am trying to find the energy to get up, maybe I'm ill, It's probably just the heat and my tiredness.	Some more interesting language choices in places might help, as might more imaginative use of figurative language.
I look again at the outline of the wardrobe and the light around the curtains. It might be getting a little lighter outside. The birds are singing happily just like they do every morning.	The answer is under the word count and the paragraphing is not fully secure.
I reech my hand out and feel for my Glasses. They might be on the bedside table. My fingers reach for them but they're not there.	
I can feel the Wood of the table and the base of a metal table light it feels cool.	20/24 marks
I look again at the outline of the wardrobe and the curtains. I can still hear the birds singing. I know I need to get up but it's warm and I don't feel too well.	Writing: 8/20 marks Style and technical: 12/20 marks

Example student response	Examiner comments
I go back to sleep for a bit and have some dreams. When I wake up again it seems a bit lighter, and I feel a bit better, so I decide to get up. I can hear the birds singing. again outside.	

2 Write about 350–450 words on the following question.

Up to 16 marks are available for the content and structure of your answer and up to 24 marks for the style and accuracy of your writing.

Describe the first day of the school year.   [40]

Example student response	Examiner comments
Students are swarmed towards the school gates. It's a swelteringly hot day and the sky is cloudless. Some students arrive on bikes, some are walking with friends and chatting about their holidays. There is a happy buzz about the place. Some of the younger students seem nervous as it is their first day at a new school. The older ones seem confidant and walk casually through up to the main door. They are all dressed in the same smart uniform and many have new shoes that are a little bit tight.	This response answers the task and contains some details describing events of the day. It is sequenced in chronological order and makes clear sense. There are a few interesting word choices and an attempt to use figurative language.
On the way to school I thought about the previous school year. I enjoyed that most of the time, but there were some days when I found school hard. Fortunately, I had some help from tutors and my parents and I managed to get better at school, especially maths. By the end of the year, I was much more confident. So as I am going to school now, I am happier and I was quite excited for the year ahead.	The second paragraph is not really describing the first day – it is more of an account
	Spelling is accurate with some exceptions ('confidant', 'seams', anacdotes'). Punctuation is accurate.
The bell rung and students head for their classrooms. In one classroom, the teacher stands up to talk. He greets his new class and smiles. He is dressed smartly in a suit with a tie. He seams kind. A girl called Tasnim raises her hand and asks the teacher a question about lunchtime. He answers and Tasnim is grateful. The classroom is decorated in a very colourful way, with a blaze of artwork on the walls. There are several computers dotted around the classroom, and a large screen where the teacher projects information.	There are issues with mixed tenses – the response changes between present and past tense at times.
	The student could focus on specific details more closely and use language in a more interesting way to convey the nature of the scene. The response could also be improved by including more on the feelings of the day.
During the day, the school is busy. In the staff room at break time, teachers ask each other about their holidays. They chat happily like bees in a hive and swap anacdotes. When the bell rings again, they went back to their classroom. One of the younger children feels a bit unwell, so his friend takes him to see a teacher. Another student seems very loud and excitable. He is tall with black hair and bright eyes. The teacher has to speak to him about his behaviour. The boy apologies and calms down. At the end of the day, everybody goes home tired but happy.	27/40 marks Writing: 11/20 marks Style and technical: 16/20 marks

3 Write about 350–450 words on the following question.

Up to 16 marks are available for the content and structure of your answer and up to 24 marks for the style and accuracy of your writing.

Describe a person you admire. [40]

Example student response	Examiner comments
A person I really admire is my brother, Joe. He is two years older than me and has always been kind and caring towards me – well, most of the time! Joe is only small, but he has a big heart. He helps out at home a lot and is very respectful towards our parents. Joe is 17 and I am 15. He has been a big influence on me. I look up to him and want to be like him. No matter what I need help with, Joe will assist. Last year, I was struggling with some maths work, so Joe spent an evening with me showing me how to use a scientific calculator properly.	This response feels more like an account than a description, but it does offer ideas about the writer's brother and presents some details. It is under the word count and its relative brevity makes it hard for the student to demonstrate their ability to sustain and structure a long response.
Another reason I like Joe is because he is good at sport. He doesn't like cricket, but he is great at football and plays for a local team. Last week, I went to watch him play. He looked very powerful as he ran down the wing in the green and white strip. He is a very selfless player and makes some really good passes. Next year, I think Joe might be made captain. He deserves it as he always encourages other players and takes responsibility.	The writing is ordered, and the spelling is accurate. To improve, it needs to offer more in the way of description by including more details about Joe's appearance and personality, perhaps by placing him in another situation, or extending the section about the football match.
A final reason I admire Joe is because he never gives up. He's good at most things at school. But finds English hard at times. Joe knows it is important to do well in English, so he found a tutor and has been working very hard. I know that he will succeed because he is determined. There have been one or two times when Joe and I have fallen out, but the majority of the time, we get on really well	25/40 marks Writing: 10/20 marks Style and technical: 15/20 marks

4   Write about 350–450 words on the following question.

Up to 16 marks are available for the content and structure of your answer and up to 24 marks for the style and accuracy of your writing.

Write a story with the title, 'The hill'.   [40]

Example student response	Examiner comments
When I was younger, my friend Sam and I used to stand at the foot of Jacob's Hill and look up. Jacob's Hill was just at the edge of our village, and it was a popular spot with tourists and some of the older boys from school. We always called it 'the dark mountain', mainly because, to our young eyes, it was huge and it seemed frightening. One day we promised to climb it together. We used to look up at the tiny figures wondering what it was like to stand at the peak and look down.	The central idea of this story is good and has great potential – two young people wanting to achieve something and failing, but then later tasting success.
One summer morning, Sam and I decided to climb the hill, even though our mothers had told us not to. We met early – 7 a.m. – and brought food and drinks with us in backpacks. The sun had risen an hour earlier, so the village was bright and rosy. The gardens looked beautiful as we passed. There were a few people leaving for work, but most people were still their houses.	The phrasing is clear, and spelling, punctuation and grammar are accurate.
As we walked both Sam and I were nervous, even if we didn't admit it. I wondered in my head whether we were doing the right thing. I knew I should have listened to my mother, but I needed to climb that hill and see the view. I was also afraid that we wouldn't have the energy to climb the hill, and that we would have to turn back half-way. And in fact, that's exactly what happened. As we got higher, the path became steeper and less easy to walk. We stopped, had a drink and then both turned round, returning home with a sense of failure. We forgot all about our desire to climb the hill.	The tension in the description of the boys first climbing the hill is underplayed – more could be made of it. More too could be made of their sense of failure.
	The part where they finally reach the top could be made more emotional – as if the idea of the climb is a metaphor for growing up.
Fifteen years later, Sam and I both returned from university. We had a spare morning and decided to finally climb that hill. Now we were older, the hill looked so much smaller. We were at the top in no time. We'd done it. As we looked down, we could see our childhood village. We walked back down feeling we'd achieved a childhood ambition at long last.	It would be possible to improve this response by adding some more interesting phrasing, dialogue and figurative choices, especially in the descriptions of the scenery and the friends' feelings.
	31/40 marks
	Writing: 12/20 marks
	Style and technical: 19/20 marks

5 Write about 350–450 words on the following question.

Up to 16 marks are available for the content and structure of your answer and up to 24 marks for the style and accuracy of your writing.

Write a story that begins with the words, 'There was no reply.'   [40]

Example student response	Examiner comments
There was no reply we'd been trying to reach base camp for several hours now, but the blizzard was swirling and the signal was non-existant. Every time I tried the radio, there was nothing – just a crackling sound.	This is a dramatic story that offers really good potential for an exciting narrative.
We are stranded here on this side of the mountain for what seemed like days but was actually around three hours. Looking back I blamed myself for leading this expedition despite being warned of its dangers by many voices at base camp. They said that the whether was about to turn, and that nobody with any sense would climb the mountain that day but I didn't care I was young and reckless at least, that's what people told me and now we were sat here, the snow swirling, and Carter with his broken leg.	It has a good story shape in that it features a difficult problem, increasing tension, and a resolution.
The accident had happened not far from the summit. As the weather closed in, Carter had lost his balance and fell. The snow gave him a soft landing, but he'd landed with his leg caught under him. By the time we reached him, battling through the blizzard, he was moaning in agony. It was clear he'd broken his leg. Fortunately, we had some medical supplies – enough to dull his pain – but I knew he needed to get to hospital soon. The pain could be managed for a while, but the cold was potentially lethal. I looked at Carter. He was brave, and was trying to make jokes, but I could see the fear in his eyes.	Improvements could be made to the different phases of the story. For instance, Carter's pain and the increasing isolation of the expedition could be developed to increase tension. Likewise, the climax where Smith arrives happens too quickly.
I tried the radio yet again. It was just a crackle. The snow seemed endless, and it was so cold. I thought about the people at base camp. Whether they heard my first call for help. Whether right now, they'd sent rescuers. I sat next to Carter and tried to keep his spirits up. I offered him some chocolate and the others in the expedition formed a shield around him to try to protect him from the cold.	Although the spelling, punctuation and grammar are mainly accurate, more could be done with description, perhaps including some figurative language to describe the conditions. The character of Carter is also flat. Some dialogue may help to characterise him further.
Suddenly, I heard a voice from the blizzard, it was Doctor Smith from base camp. There were others with him, carrying a stretcher. We were saved!	27/40 marks Writing: 11/20 marks Style and technical: 16/20 marks

6 Write about 350–450 words on the following question.

Up to 16 marks are available for the content and structure of your answer and up to 24 marks for the style and accuracy of your writing.

Write a story with the title, 'The memory'. [40]

Example student response	Examiner comments
The fire was devastating. Even though it happened twenty years ago, it exists as a very painful memory, one that's never far from my mind. No matter how hard I try I'm still troubled by the memory of that night.	This is an engaging story. The main idea – the loss of something precious – is a good area for fiction, and the emotional feelings that it generates make for an interesting read.
It was a phone call from my friend at the dead of night that alerted me. When the phone rang, I knew it was something terrible. Nobody ever calls in the middle of the night with good news. 'Samira, come quick! Your studio is on fire!' I don't think I've ever got dressed as quickly. I got into my car and sped down the twisty lanes to the harbour. There, I saw a terrible sight. My artist's studio was in flames.	The spelling, punctuation and grammar are accurate. To improve this story, it would be good to develop the descriptive qualities, perhaps using some figurative language to describe the fire and the narrator's feelings.
Fire engines were there already, hosing water onto the roof of my studio. I had been there for ten years. I used it as a place to paint. Its location next to the harbour was ideal. Nobody disturbed me, and I found the coming and going of boats and people inspiring. I used to paint some of the scenery. But as I looked at the orange flames and the extent of the damage, I knew that things were bad.	A greater emphasis on the emotional aspect of the story might also help.
In the morning light, the fire brigade confirmed what I knew – that the studio had been destroyed. I could cope with the loss of a building. My insurance would cover that. What upset me the most was the loss of my paintings. Over the years, I'd made many paintings, including some of my own family members. All that was left were blackened canvases and water-damaged frames. It was heartbreaking. It took some time before the building was demolished. It took even longer for it to be rebuilt. I watched it being reconstructed, often sitting at the harbour watching the builders make a new space for me to paint.	Experimenting with a wider range of sentence structures and punctuation would also help to demonstrate variety. A different ending may also be interesting to experiment with – one where things end happily. 32/40 marks Writing: 13/20 marks Style and technical: 19/20 marks
After what seemed like an age, I entered the new building. It felt new, clean and uninspiring. The clutter and atmosphere of the old studio was an inspiration. The new one seems absent somehow. Over the next few months, I tried to make the new studio more homely, but in the end, I realised, it was impossible.	

❯ Acknowledgements

The authors and publishers acknowledge the following sources of copyright material and are grateful for the permissions granted. While every effort has been made, it has not always been possible to identify the sources of all the material used, or to trace all copyright holders. If any omissions are brought to our notice, we will be happy to include the appropriate acknowledgements on reprinting.

Text 1.1 adapted from MyCanadaTrips.co.uk; Text 1.4 abridged excerpt from the article 'Forty years of the internet: how the world changed forever' by Oliver Burkeman, published 23 October 2009, reproduced by permission of Guardian News & Media Ltd; Text 1.6 extract from *The Island of Missing Trees* by Elif Shafak, published by Viking, copyright © Elif Shafak 2021, reprinted by permission of Penguin Books Limited; Exam Practice 2 Text A abridged from the article 'Overtourism in Venice' by Rob Perkins, reproduced by permission of Responsible Travel; Text 4.2 and 4.7 extracts from *Africa Bites: Scrapes and Escapes in the African Bush* by Lloyd T. Camp, used by permission of the author; Text 4.5 extract from the article 'Inside Petra, Jordan: Exploring the Ancient City Built by the Nabateans', reproduced by permission of Wonders Travel and Tourism; Text 4.6 and Topic 4.4 Q2 Extracts from *Butter* by Asako Yuzuki, translated by Polly Barton, 4th Estate, an imprint of HarperCollins Publishers, 2024; Text 5.7 extract from 'Dead Men's Path' from *Girls at War and Other Stories* by Chinua Achebe, Doubleday, 1973, thanks to The Wylie Agency

Cover Pchyburrs/Getty Images